ARMS CONTROL
IN INTERNATIONAL
POLITICS

ARMS CONTROL IN INTERNATIONAL POLITICS

David V. Edwards
The University of Texas

HOLT, RINEHART AND WINSTON, INC.

New York   Chicago   San Francisco   Atlanta   Dallas
Montreal   Toronto   London   Sydney

To J. Earle Edwards, Sr., in memory;
and J. Earle Edwards, Jr.,
for their examples

Preface

I undertook this study because I was convinced that although much attention had been given to particular measures of arms control such as the nuclear testban and the ban on nuclear weapons in space, inadequate attention was being given to the political requirements of these and any other arms control arrangements which might be sought. As with any public policy problem of such obvious importance, immediate issues and proposals monopolize attention not only of officials but also often of scholars. The result has been that the political problems have often been ignored by some and overestimated by others, and the most promising opportunities for arms control have often gone unnoticed. In this study I attempt to uncover and analyze these problems and the concomitant opportunities, and then to project these conclusions in an effort to determine the likely prospects for arms control arrangements in the coming decade.

No one engaged in such an uncertain operation can be unaware of the hazards of prediction. But no one concerned with the major security issues of our time can afford to be intimidated by them either. Only extensive efforts to develop insights and apply them to our problems offer grounds for hope that the future may be preferable to the past.

I wrote the first draft of this study while spending a stimulating year at the Washington Center of Foreign Policy Research in 1964–1965. Its directors, Arnold Wolfers and Robert Osgood, and my associates there—particularly George Liska and Robert W. Tucker—not only let me participate in weekly round table meetings and frequent informal conversations, but (often inadvertently) contributed to this study's development even when their sympathies were not with my pursuits. While this version of the book was completed in the fall of 1967, it anticipated the negotiation of a nonproliferation agreement, and other subsequent events seem to confirm the accuracy of its analysis.

Subsequent drafts have evolved in the course of my teaching at The University of Texas and have benefited from the comments of James E. King, Morton Halperin, Stanley Hoffmann, Samuel Huntington, and Robert Osgood, each of whom generously read and criticized one or another draft. It is unlikely that any of them would recognize this version—nor, perhaps, would any care to, for I have not always been able or willing to accept their much appreciated but often varying suggestions.

I accept responsibility for this book neither lightly nor gladly, for both the strengths and the weaknesses of my work have resulted from the complex of influence and resistance in which my education and my teaching have involved me. Most of my greatest intellectual debts are clearly indicated in the text, but neither notes nor acknowledgments can express all such indebtedness.

If, as I believe, those cited above and below as well as many of my other colleagues in the field bear considerable responsibility not only for my development but also for this book, I hope that its objectives are attained to a degree that justifies their generous investment in me.

D. V. E.

Austin, Texas

Contents

PART III

THE FUTURE OF ARMS CONTROL

Introduction

In an age of monstrous weapons, gigantic military establishments, and proliferating conflicts, nations are concerned not only with providing armed forces for defense, but also with seeking ways to maintain security in the face of conflict without resorting to the employment of those forces. One way in which nations seek to maintain security without using violence is arms control. Nations have long sought arrangements to control military establishments in order to lessen the likelihood of war or to decrease its destructiveness. But our nuclear age has brought a new urgency—and new obstacles—to this quest.

This study will attempt to discover and examine the factors which might influence nations to adopt arms control and the stages by which nations might achieve such control. It will then attempt to determine what arms control measures seem likely or even possible in the coming decade and how nations might effect further arms control. An inquiry will be made into the conditions that tend toward arms control, and such inquiry will clearly suggest much about the prospects for arms control. It will also increase our knowledge of our world, particularly the nature of and trends in international politics and their relevance to important policy problems.

But how will this study be organized and conducted? If we had a satisfactory theory of international politics, it would tell us among other things under what conditions nations would seek arms control and under what conditions those national quests would combine to result in arms control outcomes. But we do not yet have such a theory, and it appears to many that the best prospects for eventually developing one lie in pursuing studies of major aspects of international politics.

Although we do not have a general theory of international politics, we do have extensive knowledge about what happens in interna-

1

tional politics and some very strong suspicions about what factors tend to matter in international politics. In a study like the one presented here, and attempt is made to combine our knowledge of international politics—particularly that of past attempts at arms control—with our general understanding of key factors in international politics. Combining these factors, we hope to develop more precise notions or propositions about the conditions under which nations will seek arms control and about the conditions under which those quests will be successful.

This study will begin with a consideration of the objectives which arms control may be intended to serve, a careful examination of the nature of arms control measures, and a brief description of the successes and failures of past attempts to achieve arms control.

Part I will be devoted to determining the conditions under which we might expect nations to be interested in arms control. Chapter 2 will examine technology and the nature of armament as the foremost material determinants, while Chapter 3 will analyze the national and international political conditions that encourage or permit nations to seek arms control.

In Part II the focus will shift from the individual nation to the collection, or system, of nations. The four chapters in this part will study the stages by which nations, interacting, approach, attain, implement, and maintain arms control arrangements. In these chapters, the major obstacles to successful arms control will be examined, especially the recurrent problems of inspection, cheating, and control. Various ways will be proposed for coping with these problems, so that nations which desire arms control might be better able to rely upon agreements than has been possible in the past.

The chapters in Part III, which conclude this study, attempt to *predict* what will happen to the factors which tend to lead nations to seek arms control and how these national quests may interact to produce arms control arrangements in the coming decade. The final chapter concludes with suggestions for further progress in the development of promising measures of arms control.

It will become clear that this study offers few certainties about arms control, but it is hoped this study will contribute to understanding the prospects for arms control and to developing ways a nation may improve those prospects if it concludes that arms control is desirable. We may thus benefit by understanding this important aspect of international relations and the political context in which it will occur, and by also becoming able to judge and propose those measures of arms control that should improve the fate of each nation and the state of our world.

CHAPTER 1

The Nature
of Arms Control

We define arms control to include unilateral and multilateral measures that are designed to restrain the military establishment of a nation or nations through national interaction. Any measure of arms control will thus be characterized by five key features:

Each nation will be exerting control over its own military establishment.

The military establishments of the adversaries will affect each other.

Arms control measures will be concerned with things military.

Arms control measures will have a restraining effect.

Arms control measures will in some way be "institutionalized" into control provisions that may, but need not, be multinational.

Clearly the first three of these features are true of any arms measure. It is the last two characteristics which should insure some measure of control over arms. But, as we shall see, the nature of that control will be heavily dependent upon the particularities of the first three characteristics.

The Role of Arms Control

Of course, the importance, promise, danger, and effects of arms control are immensely dependent upon the character of the measures undertaken. Arms control measures may vary in many respects, the most important of which are the following: (1) *comprehensiveness* (singular or compound measures); (2) *nature* (relevant provisions, such as

3

weapons, men, budgets, deployment, usage); (3) *change* (reduction, increase, alteration); (4) *scale* (large, small); (5) *generality* (unilateral self-sufficing, unilateral reciprocation-inducing, bilateral, multilateral); (6) *publicity* (tacit or explicit, open or secret); (7) *objectives* (no war, curtailed war, nonwar side-effects); (8) *elements* (administration, inspection, verification, control, adjudication, ratification, specification and elaboration, alteration, extension and termination, and others).

It is not possible or necessary to specify in most of our analysis which types of measures would have what effects. That can and must be left largely to imagination and to occasional specific analyses. In some instances, we will find it useful to presume measures of substantial control or significant disarmament to ascertain more clearly the types of effects likely. Thus, in general, the measures examined in this study will not always be those most likely to be achieved, although the concluding chapters in this book will analyze more explicitly those prospects that seem most likely.

Arms control policy can be considered an aspect of arms policy if it is remembered that arms policy is itself a part of a nation's general foreign policy, intended to contribute to the attainment of national objectives more specific and limited than deterrence, prevailance, and defense. Both the military content of arms control measures and the self-control implicit in the concept of arms control are features that arms control shares with arms policy. And many of the possible specific objectives of some arms control measures, such as avoidance of war by accident or miscalculation, are basically military objectives as well.

However, some emphases of arms control policy differentiate it from arms policy—particularly its limitation of military forces and capabilities, and its usual institutionalization through cooperation with the adversary. Thus, those elements of military policy and conduct that are characterized by limitation and cooperation, as in sanctuary war, are probably best analyzed as arms control measures. Further, arms control policy differs from arms policy in that it may serve functions beyond the scope of arms policy alone, such as fostering international amity and cooperation or contributing to domestic economic health and social demilitarization. Thus, arms control policy is probably best considered similar to and overlapping with arms policy, but potentially broader in its role and possible functions.

Arms control policy might serve the international political objectives of national foreign policy (and perhaps occasionally such domestic objectives as strengthening the democracy and economy) in several ways. The first is coping with present and anticipated problems that obstruct the attainment of objectives. Such problems would include the destructiveness of nuclear weapons, the proliferation of nuclear capabilities and instruments, and the risk of war by accident and arms racing. But arms control measures can be more constructive, creating and exploiting opportunities for cooperation and international stabilization.

In addition, there is a third function which arms control measures may have: encouraging further agreement. Just as agreements in general might be made because of their precedential effects rather than their substantive advantages, so arms control agreements might be undertaken because they encourage further, substantively desired, agreements. There are no convincing historical examples to be found in the arms control field, although the Antarctica treaty of 1959, which provided for nonmilitarization and inspection of national installations, might be justified or explained more as a statement of interest in cooperation and trial inspection than as a measure of significant intrinsic worth.[1]

There are many possible objectives that might be served by arms control measures. Most long-range national objectives—usually stated in such general terms as "welfare," "justice," "national liberty," "personal freedom," and "equality"—could be served only indirectly by arms control measures. Peace, however, is one such general goal that might benefit directly by arms control.

This objective is traditionally put as "reducing the risk of war." It might be elaborated to include threatening crises and underlying international instability. But the very term "risk of war" conceals more than it reveals about the nature of the problem with which arms control measures are intended to cope. There appear to be four clearly distinguishable elements to the "risk of war."

The first is the probability of *accident*—unforeseen outbreak of war resulting from mechanical, informational, or judgmental errors. Coping with such a danger would require measures to improve technical systems (many or most of which are already undertaken unilaterally as they are developed) or communications and other information-gathering and analyzing devices and procedures (an example of which is the "hotline," a direct telegraphic cable linking decision makers in several nations).

[1]A comprehensive study of the Antarctic question, published just before the treaty was signed on December 1, 1959, can be found in Philip Jessup and Howard J. Taubenfeld, *Controls for Outer Space and the Antarctic Analogy* (New York: Columbia University Press, 1959), especially part II, pp. 137–190.

The second aspect of the risk of war is *possibility*. Because this element concerns the capabilities of participants to wage war, it brings the focus to the kind of war envisioned, prepared for, and escalated into. It suggests measures excluding environments (such as space) and areas (such as the Antarctic and Africa or Latin America) from the military activity of adherents. And it suggests measures designed to encourage or provide "pauses" or "cooling-off" periods between crisis and explosion, during which reconsideration, negotiation, or rearmament might be undertaken.

The third component of the risk of war is *desirability*. This concerns purposeful rather than accidental war. This is surely a major, although often neglected, element in the risk of war, especially if one nation has particularly good active and passive defense capabilities or a promising first-strike disarming attack capability. The danger arising from possession of such capabilities might be met or pre-empted by agreements constraining defense, such as those proposed to prohibit frenetic development of ballistic missile defense systems or blast and fall-out shelters, or by agreed or unilateral development of invulnerable second-strike capabilities able to overcome such defenses. In effect, such agreements would achieve deterrence by threat of punishment, which would make war a less desirable national policy.

The final aspect of the risk of war is *acceptability*. This applies to the extent to which a nation will be willing to accept war as a "necessary" cost of attaining national objectives. This is differentiated from desirability of war because "desirability" implies or suggests initiation; "acceptability" suggests willingness to run the risk should the adversary opt for war. The measures that might undermine this acceptability of war are similar to those controverting its desirability.

The other widely recognized possible objective of arms control measures is *reduction of destructiveness* if war should come. Of course "destructiveness" should be taken to denote many possible undesirabilities of war, such as extent, violence, nature, nonmilitary penetration, and "dirtiness." Among general approaches to such limitation are measures of passive defense (shelters, evacuation, and other efforts to protect people and civilian property); disarmament, which cuts back nations' war-making capabilities; and understandings to control the escalation of limited war. However, it is possible that measures taken to reduce the destructiveness of war may inadvertently reduce the undesirability and unacceptability of war and thereby obstruct the attainment of the first fundamental objective of arms control. This consideration underlies much of the continuing debate over the merits of civil defense, just as in allied military strategy it underlies the dispute between Americans and Europeans over the relative merits of increased conventional strength in Germany and the rest of Western Europe.

An alternate and more general statement of many of these objectives is *control of the arms race*. If the term "arms" is taken in a very broad sense, one aspect of such control is curtailing the scope, size, nature, cost, and risk of the military establishment. The other is controlling the speed of arms escalation by means of the interaction examined above. But those who select such a general statement of objectives would probably then decide which aspects of the arms race to control by referring to the dangers we have examined. And they would be apt to seek to create or restore some kind of balance or stability in the international military situation to avert wars and crises, whether premeditated, preventive, or pre-emptive.

This proposition of balance or stability as a desirable feature of international military postures raises the grave difficulty of providing or establishing a norm, or "objective" standard, by which to judge and delineate existing and anticipated relative international military postures. There are many varying concepts of stability, for stability may be conceived as static or dynamic, as present or future, as characteristic of a single component (or subsystem) or characteristic of a system of components, and as relative to national postures or relative to their competitive interaction. What concept of stability we adopt for this purpose depends upon what kind of international order and intercourse we desire and what we fear. These are determinations that must be made before we can design and accept arms control measures intended to stabilize the military environment and control the arms race.

Then, too, there are other objectives toward which arms control measures might contribute. One possibility—often overlooked because concentration upon adversaries characterizes military affairs—is effect upon allies. The most legitimate arms control manifestation of such an objective is the prevention of "catalysis," one nation' initiating a conflict and drawing in an ally by deceit or by activation of commitments. But arms control measures might also be undertaken for the more purely political objectives of rewarding and punishing allies. The nuclear testban treaty certainly had consequences of this type. The British (particularly the then-governing Conservative party) were especially happy about attainment of the treaty agreement, while the French and the Communist Chinese were explicitly opposed and resisted pressures to sign it, thereby presumably losing favor with their allies and prestige with the nonaligned. There is also the possibility that allies as well as adversaries will eventually be "punished" if they develop nuclear weapons capabilities, as suggested by those who advocated punishing Communist China by destroying her test sites and reactors. Agreements to undertake or sanction such activities would be arms control measures of a particularly violent sort.

There also may be internal reasons for advocating or accepting arms control agreements, such as the political fear of the garrison state; the economic disapproval of the cost, dislocation, and international financial imbalances that occur when a nation arms; or the social fear of the militarization of society and the moral disapprobation of production of all or some weapons or of the threat or use of force. In addition, there may be objectives of affecting the nation's international standing by making "phony" proposals for propaganda, prestige, favor, or other increments—something which many would argue has characterized all or most arms control negotiations since the invention of arms or the calling of conferences.[2]

These then are the major prominent national objectives toward the attainment of which arms control measures might contribute. But what sorts of measures might be available for adoption? This will depend heavily upon imaginative thought about the opportunities inherent in the five key essential features of all arms control measures.

The Characteristics of Arms Control

SELF-CONTROL

The first and most obvious feature of arms control measures is the national capacity for self-control. Military organizations have always sought control over the command, the employment, and the effects of their own armed forces; and their civilians, where they have been recognized and accepted as superiors, have usually in turn sought control over the military establishment.

[2]This view is well exemplified in John W. Spanier and Joseph L. Nogee, *The Politics of Disarmament: A Study in Soviet-American Gamesmanship* (New York: Praeger, 1962). A less incredulous view is taken by Bernard Bechhoefer in *Postwar Negotiations for Arms Control* (Washington, D. C.: Brookings, 1961). Also quite useful are the very detailed studies undertaken by the RAND Corporation, notably Cirro Zoppo, *The Issue of Nuclear Test Cessation at the London Disarmament Conference of 1957: A Study in East-West Negotiation* and *Technical and Political Aspects of Arms Control Negotiation: The 1958 Expert's Conference* (RM-3286-ARPA. Santa Monica, Calif.: RAND Corporation, 1962).

INTERACTION

The second defining characteristic of arms control measures is interaction. The nature and employment of one nation's armament has always affected that of other participants in armed conflict. The earliest manifestation of this effect is consciousness that one's military establishment affects one's adversary's, just as the adversary's military establishment and its use affects one's own.[3] Subsequent refinement of this consciousness takes into account one's own effect upon the adversary in the construction and employment of one's military establishment. Thus, if a nation seeks peace with other nations, it may attempt to design its military so that it appears to be defensive rather than offensive. Closely related to this is the third manifestation of this interaction: purposive inducement of desired behavior by the adversary, capitalizing upon the reciprocal effects of military systems and actions.[4]

When interaction takes place directly between nations, discourse about arms control is generally couched in national terms. It is clear, however, that groups of nations (such as alliances or international organizations like the United Nations or bodies created to administer and control the military establishments of constituent nations) also become important actors in arms control.[5] Furthermore, although arms

[3]See any historical analysis of war, such as Theodore Ropp, *War in the Modern World* (Durham, N.C.: Duke University Press, 1959); or J. F. C. Fuller, *The Conduct of War: 1789–1961* (London: Eyre & Spottiswoode, 1961). Note also standard works on military strategy and the comprehensive collection of essays edited by Edward M. Earle, *Makers of Modern Strategy* (Princeton, N. J.: Princeton University Press, 1941); also, the historical study by B. H. Liddell-Hart, *Strategy* (New York: Praeger, 2d. rev. ed., 1967).

[4]Particularly useful among the multitude of recent works on contemporary military strategy are Bernard Brodie, *Strategy in the Missile Age* (Princeton, N. J.: Princeton University Press, 1959); Herman Kahn, *On Thermonuclear War* (Princeton, N. J.: Princeton University Press, 1961); and Glenn Snyder, *Deterrence and Defense* (Princeton, N. J.: Princeton University Press, 1961). Focusing on the theory of deterrence, these books are grounded upon recognition of this interaction effect. Interaction as a fundamental social fact or practice is analyzed in Kenneth E. Boulding, *Conflict and Defense: A General Theory* (New York: Harper & Row, 1962); Anatol Rapoport, *Fights, Games, and Debates* (Ann Arbor, Mich.: University of Michigan Press, 1960); and Thomas C. Schelling, *Strategy of Conflict* (Cambridge, Mass.: Harvard University Press, 1960). Each of these three authors acknowledges considerable debt to Lewis F. Richardson, whose pioneering inquiries resulted in two posthumous books, *Arms and Insecurity* and *Statistics of Deadly Quarrels* (Chicago, Quadrangle, 1960).

[5]Perhaps the clearest indication of the operative existence of an international actor is the absence of a unanimity provision in the decision procedures of an international organization. Thus, the Security Council without the Uniting for Peace

control may be dependent upon transnational and supranational organizations, it may also be dependent upon subnational or even nonnational organizations and individuals. Thus, significant sources of arms
supply and demand today are private manufacturers, jobbers, and
individuals (surplus buyers, mercenaries, insurrectionists, members of
the National Rifle Association, the Minutemen, and individual sports-
men). Thus, there may be need of transnational or nonnational "civil
or military servants" to administer agreements and control behavior,
although many arms control measures could, of course, be implemented
by nationals acting as nationals. And, more fundamentally, the dependence of arms control upon interaction emphasizes the importance of
individuals in arms control, for, like the political and military deterrence with which it is intimately linked, arms control must depend upon
the perceptions, thoughts, and actions of individuals—policy makers,
policy selectors, and policy executors—because all national decisions
are, in this sense, individual decisions.

MILITARY CONTENT

The third defining characteristic of arms control measures is military content, which differentiates arms control measures from political
control measures. Although arms control measures may serve very
political objectives—as does all military policy—they are measures
involving the military establishment.

It is important that measures and analyses of arms control not be
bound by limited definitions of "arms." Dictionaries will define *arms* as
"weapons" and, traditionally, advocates of disarmament have been
concerned with weapons and personnel. Recent national drafts of disarmament treaties have become increasingly complex as military estab-

resolution was not in this sense an international actor, while the peace-keeping
General Assembly is. In such cases, the activities of the organization cannot be
analyzed simply in terms of the positions and actions of its constituents. Rather,
decision-making procedures themselves, considered fundamentally "technical" matters where unanimity must reign, become important. Are decisions made collectively
or by designated individuals? Is the mechanism of decision unanimity, majority,
or plurality voting? Are votes weighted? How and by whom is the agenda constructed? The outcome of an international organization's activity can depend, at least in
part, upon these provisions. There have been few analyses of this aspect of decision
making. However, see Duncan Black, *Theory of Committees and Elections* (Cambridge, Eng., Cambridge University Press, 1958), especially chap. 17, Ms. 355, and
his paper, "On the Rationale of Group Decision Making" (*Journal of Political
Economy*), 56 (1948), pp. 22–34. Also helpful is "Sincerity and Strategy in Voting" by Robin Farquharson (mimeographed paper, Nuffield College, Oxford: n.d.).
This is a manifestation of the argument in Chapter 1.

lishments have grown and as thinking about disarmament has deepened. Thus, the 1961 American disarmament proposal, "Outline of Basic Provisions of a Treaty on General and Complete Disarmament in a Peaceful World,"[6] contained sections devoted to armaments, armed forces, nuclear weapons, outer space, military expenditures, reduction of the risk of war, military bases and facilities, and research and development of military significance. And the subsequent Soviet "Draft Treaty on General and Complete Disarmament under Strict International Control,"[7] was similarly inclusive. Yet neither draft could be said to be comprehensive.

While much specification will be explicitly postponed until negotiation (and it is likely that much further specification would then be postponed until implementation), a disarmament agreement ideally should be comprehensive in its combined inclusions and conscious exclusions. This would require further and deeper attention to the nature of the military establishment than is often apparent. The following skeletal outline of a national military establishment is presented to suggest the areas that a disarmament agreement must recognize and the areas in which arms control measures might be sought. Although imaginative development of possible measures of arms control, based upon a conception of the military establishment and a typology of controls, would probably be of little profit without prior attention to possible and desired objectives of arms control, the purposive search for arms control measures will nonetheless be most productive when the possible types of control and the relevant aspects of the military establishment are in mind. For the purposes of arms control analysis, five categories of the national military establishment should be distinguished: weapons, personnel, resources, administration, and operations.

1. *Weapons.* For large-scale disarmament, weapon systems, such as the American Polaris, Minuteman and other shorter-range ballistic missiles, or the F-111 tactical fighter, must be dealt with. However, limited measures might well be concerned with smaller arms or components of the larger systems, such as nuclear warheads. In addition, arms control might concern specific munitions, such as weapons-

[6]USACDA, *Blueprint for the Peace Race: Outline of Basic Provisions of a Treaty on General and Complete Disarmament in a Peaceful World,* United States Arms Control and Disarmament Agency, Washington, D. C., 1962. Reprinted in the *Department of State Bulletin,* October 16 (1961), pp. 650–654.

[7]U.S.S.R., "No Arms—No Wars," a draft treaty submitted by the U.S.S.R. (Moscow: Foreign Languages Publishing House, 1962). Reprinted in USACDA, *Documents on Disarmament,* 1962, vol. 1, pp. 103–127.

fabricated fissionable material or napalm. Other important aspects of the weapons category include support goods, including materiel (essential equipment) and supplies; installations, including defenses, bases, armories, and construction; transport capacity for men, weapons, and support; maintenance; and, perhaps most important, communications.

2. *Personnel.* This category includes all soldiers, officers, civilians, and reserves, their numbers, terms of service, training, salary cost, and privileges, as well as recruitment and organization.

3. *Resources.* This includes, first, the nation's geographical position; second, its physical production capacity; third, the nation's possession, exploitation, stockpiling, and trade of natural resources; fourth, the nation's financial resources, including the nature and state of the economy, the financial system, and the budget; and, fifth, the nation's mental states and activities, that is, its composite will to act and its development and use of ideas through memory and invention. These five resources are not essentially military as are the others. They have more to do with what has traditionally been termed "the war potential of nations," but they are significant determinants of "the peace potential of nations" and, thus, important elements in the arms control of nations.[8]

4. *Administration.* This category includes command and control, mobilization process, doctrine (including strategy and tactics and whatever ideological elements enter), and information. The importance of each of these is clear; the possibility of their control is not.

5. *Operations.* This final category concerns the stages in military weapons development.[9] The first stage, generally called the "development" stage, embraces research (both basic and applied), exploratory developments, advanced developments, engineering developments, operational systems development (improvement of existing weapon systems), and management and support.[10] It is clear that this development stage determines the character of the over-all military establish-

[8]Klaus Knorr's study of *The War Potential of Nations* examines economic capacity, administrative competence, and motivation for war as the fundamental determinants of potential military power. See also part I of Charles J. Hitch and R. N. McKean, *Economics of Defense in the Nuclear Age,* which is devoted to "resources available for defense."

[9]For a treatment of military weapons development see Merton J. Peck and Frederic M. Scherer, *The Weapons Acquisition Process: An Economic Analysis.*

[10]See Robert S. McNamara, *Statement of the Secretary of Defense before the House Armed Services Committee,* pp. 93–111. See also J. A. Stockfish (ed.), *Planning and Forecasting in the Defense Industries.*

ment. It is also clear that it may determine the irrelevance or perilousness of arms control measures.

If the development stage is judged successful in test and evaluation and if need is present or anticipated, the next operation is adoption, which is followed by the procurement stages of budgeting and ordering. The subsequent production stage involves manufacturing and sale or designation. (In the United States, the production stage is best examined from the viewpoint of the private manufacturer, for most weapons production is undertaken by private industry under federal contract, although some production is undertaken by national arsenals, navy yards, and other installations.[11])

Weapons and other materiel received by the military establishment are then stockpiled or deployed. Both size and accessibility of stockpiles could be of significance for arms control, and the importance of deployment is obvious.

The next operations stage is particularly crucial. The employment, or usage, of weapons is a major concern of many arms control proposals. Weapons usage has, of course, always been a conscious concern of each military establishment. And the interaction of a nation's own usage with that of its adversary has been increasingly appreciated and exploited. Although the prime argument for disarmament has been that disarmament would eliminate war entirely, disarmament advocates have been quick to point out further that if conflict should occur, at least in a disarmed world it would probably be less severe. More recently, a primary objective of many arms control propositions has been to limit the destructiveness of war should it develop, mainly through elimination of weapons from arsenals and through regulations or understandings on their usage.

A final operation important to arms control is international assistance to allies, alliances, and unaligned nations, whether it take the form of weapons, materiel, personnel, administration, or resources (including economic aid, which permits the nation to transfer its own resources to military projects).

These operations—development, adoption, procurement, production, stockpiling or deployment usage, and assistance (coupled with weapons, personnel, resources, and administration)—constitute the as-

---

[11]The national economics of disarmament, which is beyond the scope of this study, is examined by fifteen scholars in Emile Benoit and Kenneth E. Boulding (eds.), *Disarmament and the Economy.* A careful and interesting study of the British situation is *The Economic Effects of Disarmament,* produced by the Economist Intelligence Unit.

pects of military content that might be included in arms control measures.

It must be remembered, however, that the real interest of this study and of arms control measures in general is not in weapons per se or even in what provisions are made for or against them; rather, it is in the nations and other actors themselves and what is done to affect them, fundamentally through operation of the interaction process.[12]

RESTRAINT EFFECT

The fourth defining characteristic of arms control measures is restraint effect. Just as its military content differentiates arms control from other international political policy, so its restraint effect differentiates arms control from purely military measures. This restraint effect of arms control measures imposes some limitation upon the military establishment of one or more nations. It is to be differentiated from what might be termed the "race effect" of competitive armament, even though it will be found that the same analytical framework could generally be applied to arms control policy making and military policy making, to the restraint effect and the race effect.[13]

Restraint, or limitation, characterizes arms control measures as a consequence of the objectives generally attributed to and promised by arms control: lessening the risk of war's occurrence and lessening the damage of war should it occur. While in certain situations increases in national armament might lessen the risk of war, such increases would not tend to lessen the damage of war should it occur. And it seems that simple increases in weaponry can be adequately treated as propositions of military policy alone. In addition, it is clear that disarmament consists in limitations upon the military establishment in the form of reduction of weaponry. But the greater similarity among objectives and complexities of limiting arms control and disarmament measures as

[12]This point is made in part by Thomas C. Schelling and Morton H. Halperin: ". . . most of the present study is concerned less with reducing national *capabilities* for destruction in the event of war than in reducing the *incentives* that may lead to war or that may cause war to be the more destructive in the event it occurs" (*Strategy and Arms Control* [New York: Twentieth Century, 1961], p. 3). However, their approach seems often to underestimate the opportunities and promises of changes in the weapons themselves.

[13]As will be suggested below, expansion of military power may also bring about restraint through its deterrent effect, and even relatively pure arms competition is not devoid of restraint. The point is that while not all producers of restraint may be considered arms control measures, all arms control measures will effect restraint of some sort.

against "purer" military measures suggests that such insistence might be repaid by the development of more general arms control analysis. Should this analysis prove useful when dealing with limiting arms control and disarmament, efforts might then be made to apply it to nonlimiting arms measures as well.

INSTITUTIONALIZATION

The fifth characteristic of arms control is institutionalization. There are various ways in which arms control measures might be institutionalized. The clearest type of institutionalization is explicit agreement reached through traditional diplomatic methods, as used for the nuclear testban treaty. Another widely recognized type of arms control is tacit agreement compounded of reciprocal interaction, such as the concomitant defense budget reductions announced in 1964 by the United States and the Soviet Union. Less widely recognized as arms control are measures consisting of recognized and accepted unilateral actions, such as the American program of hardening its missiles to make its military force and posture less provocative, thereby bringing about an interaction of expectations. Thus this American program was subsequently followed by a comparable Soviet program, although it did not depend upon such adversary response for its effectiveness.

"Institutionalization" is defined as the act of converting policy into practice. The behavior in question may be common or reciprocal action by several nations, or unilateral action by one nation followed by comparable action or at least abstention from reprisal by another. We explain such behavior as recognition of a mutual interest in cooperation on arms control within limits. Thus, we shall consider recognized and accepted unilateral actions that limit a military establishment to be arms control measures, institutionalized by the processes of unilateral action and responsive acceptance.[14] Such measures may differ not only in the nature of their explicitness and their reciprocality, but also in their inclusiveness, in terms of limitation provisions as well as other elements of an international agreement.

There are many possible elements of arms control measures. One provision is a statement of the objectives of the agreement. Equally preliminary is a statement of the organization—that is, what nations will participate, under what auspices, and in what roles (as sovereign independent states, as members of an alliance, as friendly nations, or otherwise). Another element is provision for administration of the

---

[14]The processes by which these various types of arms control measures are approached and attained will be examined in detail in Chapters 4 and 5.

agreement. The most widely recognized element is the statement of required and promised action or inaction or both. There are likely to be additional provisions for inspection and verification, as well as "control" provisions, which could profitably be broken down into "regulation," "enforcement," and "sanction." Provisions for adjudication of disputes under the agreement might be included. Ratification prescriptions must be included, probably with provisions for extension and termination of the agreement. And, in an agreement intended to persist over a significant time, provisions for elaboration, specification, and alteration might be included.

These proposed elements will be examined in some detail in later chapters. Of particular interest here, however, are the natures of possible provisions for the control of national military establishments. There are four basic types:

1. *Prescribed revelation of information.* Information about the nature and activity of national military establishments plays an important role in the security policy of any nation through interaction. Revelation of information has long been considered an important aspect of arms control measures in providing verification of compliance. Most recently, efforts to prevent surprise attack and pre-emption have centered upon revelation itself as an arms control measure. And the recent tacit, reciprocated cutbacks in military budgets and fissionable materials production have clearly depended upon information about military establishments released by each side with the hope of inducing reciprocation. Information released by agreement might well concern any aspects of the military establishment: weapons, personnel, resource allocation, administration, and operations. The possible opportunities for reciprocal arms control through information are great, whether it be published or its acquisition encouraged.

2. *Prescribed military postures.* Probably the most commonly conceived arms control measures include the provision of quantitative and qualitative criteria governing the numbers and types of men, weapons, and other aspects of the military establishment. But these general terms tend to obscure the various possible types of limitations that might be placed upon the military.

First, they tend to neglect certain *qualitative* restrictions. It is difficult to select tenable and desirable distinctions among weapons and postures. Efforts to do so are often based upon the distinctions between offensive and defensive or between aggressive and non-aggressive. Most recent distinctions have been made between first-strike, second-strike, and other-strike, or even between countermilitary, counterpopulation, and countercivilization. Attempts at such distinctions in arms control proposals have been studied and found to be both difficult to sustain and subject to intense political controversy, over such concepts as "aggression" or "status quo."[15]

Second, the relatively pure and popular disarmament and arms control positions obscure various types of limitation and elimination that might be sought. Levels or sizes of armaments, personnel, and other *quantitative* aspects of the military establishment may be

a. Held constant
b. Held within specified ratios for increase
c. Held below specified ceilings
d. Held above specified floors (for nonprovocative weapons)
e. Increased to equality (in terms of specified commensurable levels or "ratios" of incommensurable items)
f. Increased to stability, balance, or some other provided objective, such as a "safer" level
g. Decreased to equality
h. Decreased to stability, balance, or some other provided objective, such as a "safer" level or a "less destructive" level
i. Abandoned
j. Proscribed ("nonarmament" in terms of a specific weapon or system or of a specific area of environment)
k. Transferred to other nations (allies, neutrals) or to organizations (alliances, international organizations)

This list includes all major quantitative provisions that might be made to affect the military establishment. However, it does not indicate the various ways in which weapons quantities might be decreased, such as making weapons obsolete (through improved weapon development or defense, for example), demobilizing forces, debilitating weapons (a temporary or reversible step), and destroying weapons.

It must be recognized that these possible quantitative prescriptions, even more than the qualitative distinctions cited previously, abstract from the difficult problem of comparability of different military establishments. They constitute but the second of the archetypal "controls" that might be placed upon military establishments.

[15]See the study by Marion W. Boggs, *Attempts to Define and Limit "Aggressive Armament" in Diplomacy and Strategy,* Vol. 16, No. 1, University of Missouri Studies (Columbia, Mo.: University of Missouri Press, 1941).

3. *Proscribed allocations.* This third fundamental control, which prohibits specified allocations of economic or military resources, might include areal restrictions upon the deployment of men and weapons (that is, "nonarmament" as exemplified by the Antarctica treaty of 1959 or the 1963 space resolution passed by the United Nations General Assembly). Its greatest concern, however, is with the military use of resources, natural or financial. Measures that prescribe peaceful use of fissionable materials and charitable use of governmental funds might be considered proscribed allocations if they served to divert funds or other resources from military to civilian uses, even though they did not explicitly ban such resource allocations.

4. *Prescribed rules for action.* Rules concerned with operations, such as employment of weapons, or even the threat of such employment, and military assistance, whether they be requirements and prohibitions or only encouragements and discouragements, constitute the fourth type of control. Examples here are not hard to find: prohibition of germ warfare and regulations for the treatment of prisoners of war have previously been tried; prohibition of first use of nuclear weapons or even of aggression itself is often proposed. Regulations limiting foreign military assistance, in efforts to contain the cold war within the more "civilized" or developed continents, are a similar proposition. And regulations abolishing or forbidding alliances include another possibility.

This presentation of basic types of controls over the military establishment has abstracted from both the specific problems of each type of control and the general problems of information and control that would be integral features of any significant arms control measure. (Chapters 6 and 7 will analyze these and other problems in detail.) Delineation of the defining characteristics of arms control has included brief examination of self-control, interaction, military content, restraint effect, and institutionalization; it has allowed consideration of extensive and inclusive definitions of the terms "arms" and "control." Thus, arms control, as a concept and as a subject of political analysis, is taken here to include unilateral and multilateral measures designed to restrain the military establishment of one or more nations through interaction.

Arms Control in the Postwar Years

International disarmament agreements stand out not so much because they are significant but because they are so few and far between. The period between the Rush-Bagot agreement of 1817 (which demilitarized the Great Lakes between the United States and Canada) and the Washington Naval Agreements of 1922 featured two Hague peace conferences and a world war. Between the Washington Naval Agreements which were partially and ineffectually renewed in 1930 and Hiroshima intervened lengthy League of Nations disarmament conferences and another world war.

Postwar atomic anxiety encouraged further disarmament negotiations soon after the end of the war and the beginning of the United Nations.[16] From 1946 through 1948, discussion and negotiation concerned nuclear weapons and centered on the American Oppenheimer-Lilienthal-Baruch Plan and the Soviet alternative. The United States proposed internationalization of atomic energy, on which it then had a monopoly; the Soviet Union insisted on duplicating the American discovery while relying upon its immense superiority in conventional forces to counter American nuclear forces, which it sought to disarm. Most discussion in this period was general, and no discussion linked Western nuclear forces with Eastern conventional forces as countervailing capabilities to be controlled concomitantly. As cold-war tensions mounted and political conflict in Eastern and Central Europe developed, debate over control (which the West sought) and inspection (which the Soviets opposed) failed to become realistic, the unlikelihood of compromise became clearer, and eventually negotiation deteriorated into minimal activity. At most, these negotiations served to clarify somewhat the minimal conditions upon which each side could be expected to continue to insist.

Following accession to the "nuclear club" in 1949, the Soviet Union became increasingly intransigent. As the Soviets narrowed the American nuclear advantage and the North Atlantic Treaty Organization narrowed the Eastern conventional superiority, the importance of assessing nuclear and conventional strength together, if not necessarily considering disarmament, became clearer. Not surprisingly, each side continued to demand international reductions in the type in which it

[16]There is considerable historical literature on disarmament. The most useful works include Merze Tate, *The Disarmament Illusion* (New York: Macmillan, 1942) and *The U.S. and Armaments* (Cambridge, Mass.: Harvard University Press, 1954); Philip Noel-Baker, *The Arms Race* (Dobbs Ferry, N. Y.: Oceana, 1960); and Bernard Bechhoefer, *Postwar Negotiations for Arms Control* (Washington, D. C.: Brookings, 1961). A bibliographical guide to postwar literature can be found in Bechhoefer, pp. 601–608. Selected references to interwar literature, including bibliographies, are to be found in the Senate Foreign Relations Committee's *Disarmament and Security: A Collection of Documents 1919–1955* (Washington, D. C.: U. S. Government Printing Office), pp. 1002–1026.

was inferior. New proposals embodying concessions by each side were produced occasionally from late 1954 to late 1957 in the form of the first comprehensive plans for general disarmament. While these plans emphasized the interrelation of nuclear and conventional forces, they also manifested the Western desire to prevent the Soviets from equalling Western nuclear stockpiles and the concomitant Soviet desire to retain its intelligence advantage over the West through preservation of its closed society. Opposing positions could nonetheless be described as closer, in that the West began to recognize the importance to the Soviets of control strictly limited by veto power and the Soviet Union, now a nuclear power, became willing to postpone the control of nuclear weapons to a late stage in disarmament.

On May 10, 1955, the Soviets set forth a plan that appeared to many observers to accept much if not most of the previous Western conditions for major disarmament—a move to which the United States responded by placing a reservation on all of its previous proposals, purportedly because America increasingly realized that detection of nuclear stockpiles would prove a monstrous task and intended further to emphasize the "open skies" inspection to be propounded by President Eisenhower at the Geneva summit conference that July. Some saw in this refusal by the West to respond favorably to the Soviet proposals the passing of the one auspicious possibility of agreed general and substantial disarmament in the postwar period. Others, less sanguine at the time, have emphasized that increasing problems of inspection and the continued differences over control requirements would have prohibited agreement even then and even on these terms.[17]

[17]Philip Noel-Baker, a long-standing analyst and proponent of disarmament who could only be termed an optimist, calls his historical presentation of the Soviet proposals "The Moment of Hope" (*The Arms Race*, chap. 2). John Strachey, another Laborite less generally optimistic, remarked: "I cannot help feeling that 'the moment of despair' would be a more appropriate title. For here we have proof that even when a broad and comprehensive offer of disarmament is made by one side, and then accepted by the other, the only result is to make the sponsors of the offer withdraw in confusion" (*On the Prevention of War* [London: Macmillan, 1942], p. 157). Other analysts have been more skeptical. Pessimists John Spanier and Joseph Nogee conclude that, "As an example of gamesmanship, the Soviet proposals of May 10 ranked high indeed. For while the Soviet Union was publicly conveying the impression that it was eager for disarmament and more than willing to match the West's 'concessions,' it also attached the necessary joker provisions to ensure the rejection of its proposals." They found three. (*The Politics of Disarmament: Study in Soviet-American Gamesmanship* [New York: Praeger, 1962], p. 88.) A more balanced and more thoughtful yet still pessimistic assessment is Bernard Bechhoefer's in his *Postwar Negotiations for Arms Control*, chap. 13.

What was happening, in the subsequent assessment of an American negotiator, was that "both the Soviet Union and the West, because of developments in military technology, were shifting their emphasis in the disarmament negotiations from 'comprehensive disarmament,' which became an ultimate objective rather than an immediate program, to 'partial measures.' "[18]

By December 1957, when the Soviets refused to participate further in the Disarmament Commission negotiations, the parties had already discussed air and stationary ground inspection, zones of limited armament (the Rapacki Plan and disengagement variations), and a ban on nuclear testing.

As each side improved its posture in the other's advantageous weaponry, the strategic balance was coming increasingly to hinge upon means of delivering both nuclear weapons by airplane and rocket, and conventional forces by ground transport and airlift. Following the first testing of a Soviet intercontinental ballistic missile and the launching of Sputnik I in the fall of 1957, negotiations on general disarmament ceased. In 1958, conferences on a nuclear test suspension and on measures to prevent surprise attack were held. Also in 1958, the achievement of a moratorium on nuclear testing and the collapse of the surprise-attack talks (which the Soviets considered political and the Americans treated as technical) bespoke the new and increasing emphasis upon partial measures of arms control.

But partial successes were followed by further failures on an expanding scale. At the United Nations General Assembly in September 1959 both the British and the Soviets produced proposals for "general and complete disarmament" in three stages, and the Americans followed with their proposal the next spring. When the Soviets walked out of the talks in mid-1960, negotiation was suspended until March 1962, when the still-functioning Eighteen-Nation Disarmament Conference was constructed of five Western, five Eastern, and eight nonaligned nations. The talks were notable both for the developing agreement once again to allow possession of nuclear missiles into the later stages of disarmament and for the continued refusal of France, one of the eighteen members, to participate. This refusal, coupled with the continued exclusion of Communist China, renders the discussion of general and comprehensive disarmament unpromising.

Progress on limited measures has been achieved, however, in smaller and less formal bodies. In December 1959, the demilitarization

[18]Bernard Bechhoefer, *Postwar Negotiations for Arms Control*, p. 314.

of the Antarctic was agreed to by the twelve countries with claims in that territory. This treaty was significant in its elimination of the imminent possibility of competitive armament in the Antarctic and in its allowance of untrammelled inspection by and of all parties in the Antarctic.

The limited nuclear testban treaty of July 1963 resulted from talks beginning in autumn 1958 under the moratorium and continuing sporadically until suddenly in June 1963 the Soviets indicated willingness to consider an American proposal of August 1962, for an agreement excluding underground tests, which the United States maintained were potentially undetectable. The Soviet turnabout is often explained in terms of the post-Cuban missile crisis quest for *détente* and as an effort to embarrass China. Once political conditions and considerations warranted or suggested such an agreement, it was easily reached.[19]

The agreement establishing a direct telegraphic link (or "hotline") between the United States and the Soviet Union, based upon an idea which appears to have originated in the early 1960s when American strategists were concerned with the possibility of major war by misinformation or miscalculation, was signed in June 1963, although the development of invulnerable deterrent forces had already substantially reduced the danger of pre-emptive attack.

The possibility of competitive militarization of space was met by a General Assembly resolution banning the orbitting of nuclear weapons, which was passed unanimously in October 1963, following some six years of sporadic discussion. This was an arms control provision undertaken before threat had materialized or had been substantially lessened by conditions. And although the agreement did not provide sanctions, it was one in which sanctions seemed less important than mutual assurances that neither side would undertake actions that would be costly, provocative, and unlikely to be useful if duplicated.

The attainment of these four limited measures (Antarctic nonmilitarization, the limited testban, the "hotline," and the nonmilitarization of space), which were accompanied by reciprocated reductions in defense budgets and in production of fissionable materials in 1963 and 1964, suggests the possibility of agreement on further partial measures,

[19]Clearly the limited nature of the treaty, providing for no inspection and for withdrawal with warning, contributed to the ease of its attainment. The fact and experience of five years of negotiations on nuclear test suspension were also significant. The treaty and its provisions will figure prominently in the forthcoming chapters.

PART I

The Determinants
of Arms Control Policy

CHAPTER 2

Material Conditions

Technology

Whether termed the nuclear age, the missile age, or the computer age—or even the age of anxiety—this era is characterized by the products and effects of its technology. Technological development is not a new phenomenon, but the increasing rate of technological innovation that was fostered in World War II has intensified during the cold war. Under strong governmental leadership and finance, military considerations and economic incentives have encouraged the increased application of natural science to technological innovation, institutionalizing continual production of technological innovation.[1] The resulting development has been greatest in the technologies of destruction, of transportation, and of information and communication. The magnitude of possible destruction has been multiplied immensely by weapons development; the capacity and speed of transportation have been increased by improvements in airplanes and missiles; and the national capability for rapid decision making, as well as delivery of commands to both men and machines, has been greatly improved by electronics advances in instruments of data processing and of communication.

The consequences of this continuing technological development are little short of revolutionary. Just as industry surpassed demography and geography as determinants of military establishments and capabilities, so science and technology are surpassing industry. Still, the advanced technology required for nuclear, missile, and computer develop-

---

[1]See J. P. Corbett, *Europe and the Social Order* (Leyden: Sythoff, 1959), chap. 1 on "systematic innovation" and Hedley Bull, *Control of the Arms Race* (London: Weidenfield and Nicolson, 1961), chap. 12 on "the problem of continuous innovation."

ment and production cannot possibly be achieved and employed without a massive industrial base and its institutionalization of continual innovation, for the invention and production of such devices results from the distillation of the power of an entire nation.[2]

The important distinctive features of armament in the present age have resulted from nuclear, missile, and information developments. Advances in the technologies of destruction and transport have made it possible to destroy an adversary without prior defeat or disarmament. In several important senses, major war has been removed from the battlefield. The medium in which it would be fought would likely be the air, the locus of destruction would be large military and industrial complexes, and further, the decisive moves (such as deployments) would probably be undertaken in advance of military activity. The threat of annihilation without previous military defeat has fostered the incentive of pre-emption before a nuclear exchange begins (striking first when one believes that an adversary is about to strike) and the incentive of preventive escalation (raising the level of confrontation once an exchange has commenced)—each intended to eliminate or lessen the possibility of total destruction without prior defeat.

In the face of this increasing indefensibility of nations, developments in the technology of defense construction have trailed advances in the technology of offensive destruction. Efforts for defense construction have taken two forms: Construction of protection for military weapons (for example, concrete silos to "harden" missiles) has increased the survivability and hence the retaliatory capability of missile nuclear forces; and construction of shelters against fall-out and even blast from nuclear explosions shows some promise of increasing the defensibility of peoples and command centers, if not of industrial and urban complexes themselves. Nonetheless, the monstrousness of the destructive capabilities when coupled with the massiveness of the obstacles to active defense against them offers little hope that the technology of construction and defense can equal or satisfactorily cope with the technology of destruction. This mutual indefensibility increases the importance of unilateral control and reciprocal restraint in the employment of the instruments of destruction and perhaps in construction as well. It is toward such unilateral control and reciprocal restraint that arms control measures are directed.

Developments in the technology of information and communica-

---

[2]This point is made strongly by Kenneth Waltz in "The Stability of a Bipolar World," *Daedalus,* 93 (1964), pp. 881–909.

tion have created both the threat and possibility of total destruction; but also they have increased the possibility of restraint and control. The scientific and technological knowledge underlying military capabilities has always been permanent in that it could not be eliminated unless frontal lobotomies were performed on all knowledgeable men. But the development of programmed activity and protected communications since World War II has made it possible, if not necessary, for a nation to construct its military machine so that the destruction of its populace need not interfere with its destructive military operations. When such programming is employed, prewar contingency planning and development of strategy are of gravely increased importance, for in mortal national combat the brief time available to decision makers will be monopolized necessarily by choice and communication.

Technological developments in destruction and transport have increased incentives not only for programmed activity and protected communications to guarantee counterdevastation in the event of attack, but also for exploitation of the possibility of an automated response that would increase unilateral control and thereby avert escalation and destruction should mutual restraint prove possible. Hence, it is important in assessing the effects of technological development not to stop with consideration of effects upon armament as discussed above, but to move to an examination of the impact of such technology and its armament upon strategy and policy. The role—and indeed the desirability—of armament is determined not only by technology, but also by the international political context and the national policy that affect the strategy by which armament is developed and deployed. And obviously, both strategy and policy are affected by the nature of armament.

Military strategy employs military forces to achieve the ends set by political policy. The importance of the psychological and political aspects of strategy in the postwar years has been heightened by technology, which has made advanced preparation, rather than use, pre-eminent. While programmed activity has increased the importance of advance contingency planning, the destruction envisaged as an almost inescapable consequence of any major war has shifted primary attention from defense aimed at victory to deterrence aimed at military stalemate and perhaps even political stability.

Yet the inevitable uncertainty of all deterrence is enhanced by the fact that the weapons and other deterrence activities are generally untested in battle. This uncertainty exacerbates another fundamental effect of technology upon strategy: the developing threat of escalation and consequent emphasis on control. Escalation can be employed in both the threat and the use of force. The ascendance of deterrence over defense has not heralded the disappearance of war and other conflict from international relations. Rather, in effect, war is now generally "fought," prepared for, and scheduled in any by diplomatic acts rather than on the battlefield. Diplomatic activity has begun to have greater military content. Thus, for example, military demonstrations have undergone a marked change of form. Traditionally, such demonstrations were intended and understood to indicate that the demonstrating power was nearing the end of its patience and was contemplating undertaking grave measures. But more recent military demonstrations have been used with less discrimination and are now designed to indicate capability rather than intent; in short, they have become predominantly military rather than diplomatic activities.[3] The effectiveness of military demonstration has been lessened by the deterioration of its symbolic nature as well as by the increasing ambiguity of underlying national intent.

Capability is easily demonstrated by ostentatious development, testing, and deployment. But for the demonstration to be fully effective, will as well as capability must be manifest. Demonstration of will, motivation, or intent has always been difficult, but it has become even more difficult with the breakdown of the symbolic character of the military demonstration and the development of military weapons systems, which almost guarantee widespread disaster if used by both sides. This problem of making one's strategy credible through demonstration of will has led some to suggest that the decision maker appear willful and others to advocate that he manifest commitment, whether by promise, by presence, or by elimination of alternatives and escapes.

Nations cannot fight and survive a nuclear war, yet they often hold or covet territorial and political positions in many places and face or foment revolution in many others. Thus, there has been a resurgence of interest in conventional war and an increased participation in guerilla war. Emphasis upon conventional and otherwise "limited" war has been the primary strategic response of the major powers to the technological innovation of the postwar years. But the emphasis upon conventional rather than nuclear war has actually intensified the threat of nuclear war through gradual escalation. It has encouraged strategists to envision a multitude of small steps on the "escalation ladder" and at

[3]Like most of the trends and developments examined here, this has roots in the interwar years, when the Soviets declined to accept this traditional concept of the demonstration. See Alfred Vagts, *Defense and Diplomacy: The Soldier and the Conduct of Foreign Relations* (New York: King's Crown, 1956), p. 259.

the same time it has broken down the traditional distinctions between combatant and noncombatant, between the military and the civilian industrial plant of the nation, and between internal civil conflict and transnational or international war. This breakdown has been spurred by the increase in guerilla conflicts. Guerilla activities have arisen because partisan movements could fight no other war; they have become increasingly the pattern because national governments as well as outside advisers and assistants are often unable to cope with such encounters in conventional ways. Thus, the pattern has become one of foreign military aid by the major powers to smaller governments fighting internal wars, often coupled with limited engagement by one of the major powers itself in an effort to keep encounters—particularly potential major power encounters—limited.

These developments and considerations have brought about increasing reliance upon what General André Beaufre has termed "indirect strategy"—"The art of making the best use of the limited area of freedom of action left us by the deterrent effect of the existence of nuclear weapons and of gaining important and decisive victories in spite of the fact that the military resources which can be employed for the purpose must in general remain strictly limited."[4] The instruments of such indirect strategy are not nuclear weapons, but rather political and moral suasion coupled with conventional force directed at piecemeal victory or at gradual erosion.

Just as the effects of technology upon armament have been reflected in changes in strategy, so these changes in strategy are clearly related to changes in policy, which sets the ends that strategy is designed to achieve. Because strategy must be "total" now, the cost of being a major power is probably higher than ever in relation to the lesser cost of being a troublesome and perhaps catalytic lesser power. Thus, Great Britain has sought to cut its political commitments and military establishment, finding the cost of aspiring to great power status too high; on the other hand, France and Communist China have enjoyed the luxury of fomenting trouble within their alliances and now, through development of nuclear weapons, aspire to make the great leap forward to the major power camp. The success of these efforts at ascension will probably be curtailed by the smallness of the French economy and the weakness of the Chinese economy. The very existence of such multipolarizing efforts is itself in large measure a conse-

---

[4]André Beaufre, *An Introduction to Strategy* (New York: Praeger, 1965), pp. 109–110.

quence of the indefensibility of the state, which lessens the direct usefulness of tight alignment and encourages independent efforts at accommodation.

The strategic necessity of concentrating upon advanced preparation for deterrence rather than upon employment of armaments for defense can be viewed in terms of avoiding war of any kind, or at least of limiting any war to be fought. Thus, the main effect of armament upon strategy and in turn upon policy is one of constraint. And the most obvious, if not necessarily the most consequential, is the military constraint resulting from developments in the technologies of destruction and transportation.

But while the military constraint is most frequently recognized, the political restraint, which in a sense followed from the military constraint, may be the most consequential. Nations have been compelled by the danger of general war to adopt an indirect approach to their political activities; some national goals have had to be limited temporally or perhaps projected over greater time. A major nation can no longer envisage destroying another important nation, an adverse economic system, or a hated ideology without risking its own concomitant destruction. So nations must develop and rely upon indirect approaches of drift and erosion, embodied in indirect strategies of posture and maneuver. This is the essence of the effect of technology upon strategy and policy, manifest in the resort to indirect strategy or political activity.

But the risk of undesired and monstrous war persists, because the weapons upon which nations must rely for deterrence and for limited military activity—functions that armaments still may serve satisfactorily—might themselves at some point exert a greater influence upon international politics and encourage the major war that no nation wants. It is an important question, then, whether the possible consequences of development, possession, and use of weapons, particularly in this era of continual innovation and compounding destructiveness, themselves impose or encourage limits upon national military establishments, limits which imply that measures of arms control could prove beneficial and hence may serve as material determinants of national interest in arms control.

Armament

Traditionally, advocates of disarmament have argued that armaments should be curtailed or abolished because they *cause* war or because, as the means of war, they *permit* war. The contention that armament permits war ignores or dismisses the political bases of conflict and further fails to consider the likelihood that were spears abolished, men might still engage in fisticuffs. Thus, the essential impossibility of abolishing all violent means of human conflict, coupled with the consequential importance of the political basis of conflict, renders this argument against armament unacceptable—indeed, naïve and dangerous.

Not so easily dismissed is the contention that armaments actively cause war. Such argument is usually grounded upon the nature of some weapons systems or on predictions concerning the outcome of arms races; but a previous and more general point is rightly made by Hedley Bull:

It is true that, within states, armaments tend to create or to shape the will to use them, as well as to give effect to it; . . . Within each state, the military establishment, called into being by the policy of competitive armament, develops its own momentum: it creates interests and diffuses an ideology favorable to the continuation of the arms race and generates pressures which will tend to resist any policy of calling it off. In this respect, that they display a will to survive, the armed forces, the armaments industries, the military branches of science and technology and of government, the settled habits of mind of those who think about strategy and defense, are like any great institution involving vast, impersonal organizations and the ambitions and livelihood of masses of men.[5]

More specifically, it is often argued that because of the nature of the weapons held, war will be the outcome of a conflict between nations armed with nuclear weapons, ballistic missiles, and other mass-destructive and rapid-fire weapons and delivery systems. Where launch-to-impact time is less than the time required for preparation and launching, the incentive is high for trigger-readiness or pre-emptive strike (that is, anticipating an aggressive strike and prohibiting it by first strike, or at least guaranteeing counterpart destruction by launching a force before attack is received). Such a pre-emptive strike—or indeed, the more traditional preventive strike—may pre-empt not only the adversary strike, but also the possibility of last-ditch negotiation or second thoughts. And such a "responsive" strike would be a high price indeed to pay for accident, mischief, or miscalculation.

The possibility of accident has been much discussed in both popular literature and technical reports, despite military assurance that such

[5]Hedley Bull, *Control of the Arms Race,* pp. 6–7.

possibility has been satisfactorily coped with.[6] But even if one nation's forces are constructed and conducted so that accident is impossible (or virtually impossible), it would be advantageous for it to ensure that the adversary's force is also accident-free. Equally dangerous and worth serious consideration is what is sometimes referred to as "mischief"— internal sabotage and external catalysis (that is, initiation of a major power war through provocative or commitment-invoking action by a lesser power).[7] A still more serious danger is miscalculation through misinformation, misassessment, or misprojection.

Measures may be undertaken unilaterally to prevent and if necessary to absorb such misfortunes as accident, mischief, and miscalculation, as through improved radar pick-up and discrimination, improved command and control, or increased invulnerability of forces to allow later response to suspicious events. Preventive measures may also be multilateral, as through increased information sharing by joint read-out of warning systems, improved communications through "hotlines," or reciprocally increased information by exchange of inspection teams to seek evidence of military activity or its absence,[8] or even reciprocally increased informability brought about through the exchange of inspection teams whose function is to be convinced by the adversary during a crisis or after an accident that military activity is not being undertaken.[9] Some such arms control measures have been undertaken, while others remain only proposals. But all are intended, at least in part, to

[6]There are periodic accounts in the newspapers of measures undertaken unilaterally to curtail the danger of war by accident. Early technical nongovernmental studies were undertaken in the late 1950s as part of the Mershon National Security Program at Ohio State University. See especially John Phelps et al., *Accidental War: Some Dangers in the 1960s* (Columbus, Ohio: Mershon National Security Program, June 28, 1960). A stimulating analysis is found in Thomas C. Schelling, *Strategy of Conflict* (Cambridge, Mass.: Harvard University Press, 1960), pp. 188–203, 247–254.

[7]See Thomas C. Schelling and Morton H. Halperin, *Strategy and Arms Control* (New York: Twentieth Century, 1961), chap. 3.

[8]Such teams of freely roving inspectors already exist in Germany as a result of the Potsdam Agreements. Western teams are stationed in East Germany and Soviet teams work in West Germany. The most complete published material on these arrangements is in I. F. Stone, "A Hopeful Crisis Story the Government Withholds," *I. F. Stone's Weekly,* 10 (Dec. 10, 1962), pp. 1, 4. See also, "Military Liaison Missions" by Brig. W. F. K. Thompson in Evan Luard (ed.), *First Steps to Disarmament: A New Approach to the Problems of Arms Reductions* (London: Thames & Hudson, 1965), pp. 161–167.

[9]This proposal was developed by Thomas Schelling in, "Arms Control: Proposal for a Special Surveillance Force," *World Politics,* 13 (1960), pp. 1–18.

break the anticipated and feared causal link between existing armaments and war.

The other alleged causal link is between increasing armaments and war. An increase in armaments among adversaries need not constitute an arms race. Some arms competition tends to be self-limiting, facilitating or inducing benign responses by an adversary; efforts to cope with dangers of accident and surprise attack would exemplify self-limiting arms competition if they entailed military developments (such as improved command and control or hardening of missiles), which probably would not aggravate military relations. An arms race is defined as a case of interaction among states or coalitions consisting in competitive quantitative or qualitative increases in armaments or other aspects of the military establishments, such as civil defense.

Clearly there is no such thing as one kind of arms race or even a "typical" arms race. At any time, an arms race could be fundamentally quantitative or qualitative, and one arms race might be distinguishable from another by the types of arms involved, such as offensive or defensive, provocative or nonprovocative. Interactive change of military posture could be discerned in arming in past centuries; indeed, there exists considerable data about arms races since the early seventeenth century.[10] But, as Samuel P. Huntington argues, arms races have become more frequent and distinctive because of conditions particularly characteristic of the nineteenth and twentieth centuries, among them a state system that facilitates the balancing of power by internal rather than external means, the pre-eminence of military force-in-being over other factors as an element of national power, the capacity of each state to increase its military strength internally through quantitative or qualitative means, and the increased awareness by each state of the dependence of its own arms policy upon that of other nations.[11]

[10]See C. B. Joynt, "Arms Races and the Problem of Equilibrium,"*Yearbook of World Affairs 1964* (London: Stevens, 1964), pp. 23–40.

[11]Samuel P. Huntington, "Arms Races: Prerequisites and Results," in C. J. Friedrich and S. Harris (eds.), *Public Policy, 1958* (Cambridge, Mass.: Harvard University Press, 1959), pp. 41–86. Huntington also argues that arms races result when nations have relative goals of armament, determined as functions of the level or type possessed by other states, but not where nations select absolute levels or types of armament as their goals. This distinction appears relevant and useful, but it may be doubted in practice that what look like absolute goals are more than goals whose relativity is disguised by the acceptance of ranges and thresholds rather than specifications which fluctuate freely and numerically with adversary armament. Thus, Huntington cites the case of Great Britain, which "followed a relative policy with respect to the capital ships in its navy but an absolute policy with

All arms races will be constructed of increases undertaken at a tempo that implies that they are more than simply adjustments to continuing conflicting interests; there is an effective dynamic inherent in the process of increase. In these terms, a series of different types or perhaps different aspects of an arms race between any pair of actors can be distinguished:

1. The development of suspicion or hostility in policy making and diplomatic practice, which may underlie the quantum jump to arming

2. The hostile deployment, redevelopment, and other alteration of the existing military situation

3. The quantitative arms build-up, which depends upon existing technology and productive capacity

4. The qualitative arms build-up, which may be a long-run development of the quantitative build-up, occurring over years because of lead times in weapons development, or which may be the first stage in a race initiated by a quantitatively weaker nation seeking to alter the criteria of strength to the disadvantage of the reigning leader

5. The mobilization race, which took weeks before World War I and might take but days or hours now, involving competitive maneuvering for readiness and, if time permits, for position

6. The process of interacting expectations, which may lead to pre-emptive initiation

7. The process of escalation, which may raise the level of armed confrontation qualitatively or quantitatively in many various ways.[12]

---

respect to its cruisers, the need for which, it was held, stemmed from the unique nature of the British Empire" (p. 50.) In support he quotes the explanation by the First Lord of the Admiralty, Lord Goschen, to Parliament in 1896: "The number of cruisers is based not upon a comparison of the number of cruisers other nations have, because their conditions are totally different from ours, but upon the question what we have to defend, what services will have to be performed, in what direction the food supply will have to be protected, and what resources we have." But this seems to be a statement, not of an absolute goal, but of a sophisticated relative goal, recognizing that mere numbers alone should not be determinant but implying that the size of adversary armament, coupled with or limited by another fundamental factor—"what resources we have"—examined in terms of function and objective, will determine the size of the British force. The basic point is simply that, at least over time which allows for changes in armament and understanding, a nation's military establishment will be affected by and will be some function of those of other nations deemed relevant.

[12]Thomas Schelling suggested examination of mobilization, expectations, escalation, and arms build-up in his review of Boulding's *Conflict and Defense* entitled "War without Pain, and Other Models," *World Politics,* 15 (1963), pp. 465–487. The list is further expanded here because of the obvious comparabilities of the items included and their importance to arms control.

The common characteristic of these seven types of arms races is an accelerating competitiveness. Given national perceptions of competition and conflict, beliefs about the hostility of adversaries, demands for parity or superiority, desires to provide against unforeseeable breakthroughs by others, and recognition of the inevitability of lead times in weapons research, development procurement, and employment, it is surprising not that there are arms races, but rather that there are not *more* arms races and arms races of greater severity.

When national armament is unstable, it is not just because weapons technology develops and military strategy and tactics change or because adversary armament and its employment change; it is also because each nation's policy is based upon its images and beliefs about itself as well as upon its views about the images and beliefs of other nations.

While an arms race may eventuate in war, it may also terminate with nonviolent capitulation by one nation—acceptance of revised relative strengths as preferable to continued arms racing. Or the outcome may be agreement, formal or informal, to terminate the race and accept (as a somewhat stable new equilibrium) the resulting relative posture. It is also possible that the parties will agree to reorganize the whole system, either by creating a new system in which relative strength is not of recognized importance or by changing the constituents of relative strength. For example, nations might replace militant international intercourse with peaceful coexistence and competition or they might "agree" to shift attention and endeavor from offensive systems to defensive ones, thereby once again defining strength in terms of defense rather than retaliation and destruction. Such reorganization of the whole system, should it occur, is more apt to result from competitive endeavors other than arming and probably other than international. But in a sense, such reorganization is what some major arms control measures, especially those entailing major disarmament, are designed to achieve. Underlying many past propositions of general and comprehensive disarmament is the contention that if abolishing arms did not itself guarantee peace, the substitution of nonviolent for violent weapons in the diplomatic arsenals of nations would bring about a substantive change in the international system. Advocates of unilateral disarmament as a practical policy, rather than simply as a morally incumbent policy, have always rested their argument on this contention. There are limited arms control measures that might be viewed as arms races and that depend specifically on the reorganization of the system. Thus, measures designed to lessen the effectiveness of surprise attack and decrease the extent to which military effectiveness is dependent upon offensive or first-strike use (such as the dispersal of bombers or the hardening of missiles) can be seen as changing the system so that arms races of this sort need not be so mutually self-defeating and so that arms races of other sorts need not be undertaken.

Neither historical study nor contemporary analysis supports the contention that arms races generally cause wars. Huntington's careful examination of thirteen arms races concludes that "(1) War is more likely to develop in the early phases of an arms race than in its later phases. (2) A quantitative race is more likely than a qualitative one to come to a definite end in war, arms agreement, or victory for one side."[13] Arthur L. Burns's analytical examination of these conclusions generally confirmed Huntington's thesis, although it produced several qualifications.[14]

Indeed, there may be features of absolute and relative arms postures that contribute to stability and that may be attained by arms racing; in any event, the arms race is not itself an autonomous process, devoid of international and national political determinants. The limitations of the argument that arms races cause war reside partly in the concept of causality, a conceptual and philosophical problem beyond

[13]Samuel P. Huntington, "Arms Races: Prerequisites and Results," p. 79.

[14]"Huntington considers arms races as a series of alternative leaps forward. On such an assumption, and given also the offense-favoring situation . . . he is surely supported in his principal contention that 'the danger of war is highest in the opening phases of an arms race, at which time the greatest elements of instability and uncertainty are present.' He is also supported (again given his assumption of alternate leaps) in the defense-favoring situation. . . . But, if instead we assume an offense-favoring situation with sophistication on both sides, explosion into war should be more likely *later* in the race . . . (p. 63).

"Huntington's principal argument for the relative safety of the qualitative race is that each new stage of it cuts short a dangerous quantitative race to build up stocks of the former ruling weapons. In many states of military art, that argument will be valid. But I suggest that there may well be others in which it is not. . . . Before they arrive at this peaceable (but, according to Huntington, merely temporary) haven [of mutual deterrence through a balance of terror], the contestants either must pass together through the extreme dangers of the area of symmetrical first strikes or must agree (short of drastic disarmament) that one of them shall be for some time quite at the mercy of the other. . . . Our objection does not call in question his subsidiary view that the advantages accruing from a technological breakthrough are necessarily too short lived to upset the balance. Indeed, we build upon that view, correct or not, and assume only that one cannot *know* that all future innovations will generate conditions of absolute stability *within the first few years* of their production" (Arthur L. Burns, "A Graphical Approach to Some Problems of the Arms Race," *Journal of Conflict Resolution,* 3 [1959], pp. 326–342. See especially pp. 338–341).

the scope of this study. It would be accurate to say that *some* arms races have *eventuated* in war (for example, the Anglo-German naval rivalry and the Franco-German land rivalry, which preceded World War I; the Franco-German land rivalry and the Anglo-German air rivalry preceding World War II; the Russo-German land rivalry preceding the invasion of Russia; and the American-Japanese naval rivalry preceding Pearl Harbor), although there were obviously other factors to which one would wish to assign some causal role in these cases. But other arms races have not led to war (for example, the Anglo-French naval rivalry of 1840 to 1866; American naval rivalries with the Japanese prior to the Washington Naval Agreements and with the British prior to the London Agreements; and, of course, the postwar Soviet-American rivalry).[15] But although arms races cannot be considered inevitable producers of war, they must be considered expensive, potentially conducive to war, and certainly corrosive of international confidence and understanding. Thus, nations impressed by these costs will tend to be interested in arms control measures designed to prevent or curtail arms races.

A final potentially deleterious consequence of armament remains to be considered. This is the possibility that, given war as a characteristic of the state system or as the outcome of a specific international crisis, the existence of certain armaments will bring about disaster. In our nuclear age, this is a contention that needs no elaboration. But it should be recognized that the problem is not simply that nations which have such destructive weapons will use them. Indeed, as has been suggested above, it is quite likely that there would be built-in incentives for each nation *not* to use them. But conflict situations may not prove pure enough to encourage the operation of such incentives unless the incentives are elaborated or explicitly understood. Reciprocally reinforcing misunderstanding, pre-emptive escalation, and catalysis are all possible ways to destructive disaster, despite disincentives arising from the nature of the weapons.

There are various ways in which such dangers might be dealt with: for example, focusing efforts upon altering or controlling the processes of misunderstanding, escalation, and catalysis or providing in advance against disaster through active defense (such as antiballistic missiles) or passive defense (such as civil defense and evacuation). But if national attention is focused upon the armaments themselves and their use, nations may make efforts to limit the use of the weapons as

[15]These examples are among those which Samuel Huntington considered.

well as the conduct of war, both of which are traditional arms control objectives. Thus, in these terms, controls against accident, miscalculation, mischief, pre-emption, arms races, and weapons usage could be thought desirable.

Closely related to technology and armament as possible material determinants of national desire for arms control are geography, economy, and knowledge. We must consider each.

Geography

The nature and international political role of geography (defined broadly to include both relative location as well as climate and natural resources) has long been studied and is widely appreciated. Until the technological developments of the midtwentieth century, geographic position in itself was an important determinant of attitudes toward arms control. Certainly, nations have been hesitant to voluntarily disarm or to rely on an agreement to disarm against a hostile contiguous neighbor. But today, at least over a short time span and with continuing "permanent" patterns of alignment, a nation may be able to cope with geographical problems by employing technology, as has been done most notably by the major powers in their development of ballistic missiles. Similarly, geography no longer offers the protection it once did. Thus, geographic location and technology can frequently be viewed as a pair, or set, of determinants, and what impact geographic position may still have on the quest for arms control must be viewed in terms of technological development.

Climate has little or no effect on determining national attitudes toward arms control, but natural resources may have some influence. Given the necessary technology and economic resources, the quest for nuclear power will depend upon either possession of the natural resources needed for nuclear development as well as the technical competence and economic strength requisite, or political ways of obtaining assistance. But these problems tend to be more political than material.

Economy

There are two ways in which the economy may condition the national quest for arms control: It may provide a limit to possible armament that will compel a nation to seek security through agreement with allies or adversaries; or it may pose continuing questions of allocation. If there is an inherent economic limit to possible defense spending, it apparently has not been reached yet by any major power. Continued high-level arms spending, abetted perhaps by decisions to undertake major programs of active and passive defense, may uncover such national limits, at least for lesser powers; but it seems more likely that the limit upon arms spending is the point where other possible expenditures and their consequences, such as Great Societies, are preferred to more arms spending and its consequences. Both the quantitative threshold and the preference scale will differ among nations, but all nations will, in fact, face a continuing question of allocation.

It is to be expected that the arms control implications of such allocation questions will be greatest for lesser nuclear powers, such as Britain in the late 1960s and France and perhaps Communist China in the 1970s. New nuclear powers, which are not interested in nuclear limitation while they are developing their capabilities and testing their economic capacities, may become interested in nuclear disarmament that would tend to equalize all nuclear capabilities. Similarly, one would expect lesser conventional powers to seek agreements discouraging costly and reciprocally disadvantageous local arms races within their areas if they believe themselves able to have confidence in the agreements which might be achieved and if they do not fear likely political problems in their area. Nations will, however, be conscious of the cost of both the quest for and the maintenance of arms control in their assessments, just as they will probably consider both the actual and the opportunity costs of their policies. More specifically, they will weigh both the economic cost of arming and the noneconomic benefits of arms control (which together will constitute the incentive to achieve arms control) against the economic cost of arms control quest and maintenance plus the noneconomic benefits of arming (which will together constitute the incentive not to undertake arms control).

Knowledge

Another material determinant of immense importance but which is often overlooked is knowledge. If relevant and promising arms control measures and ways of achieving them have not been developed and are not known, arms control agreement cannot be achieved. The analysis of the nature of arms control has made this obvious. The analysis of the stages of arms control in coming chapters will make it specific.

Conclusion

The material conditions which have been considered in this chapter—technology, armament, geography, economy, and knowledge—are important contributors to a nation's international political plans and actions. It is clear that technology and armament are particularly important to a nation's arms control interest. But while such material factors may create or strengthen the need for arms control, it is the political factors that provide the context in which that need is felt and which will engender the necessary desire. This will be discussed in Chapter 3.

CHAPTER 3

National and International Political Conditions

National interest in arms control will depend in part upon the nature of the arms control possibilities under consideration, which in turn will depend largely upon the factors of technology and armament examined in Chapter 2. But all such consideration will take place in the context set by the international political situation, and will arise in the conduct of national politics. This chapter will analyze both the national and the international political conditions that would tend to encourage national policy favorable to arms control.

National Political Conditions

The term "political" applies to both the process of policy making and the process of competition among parties and men. In arms control policy making, interests and objectives will be determined in part by the ideologies of the leaders and of the political public. The context in which they will be determined will include opportunities and obstacles arising from the national material conditions (technology, economy, and geography), and challenges arising from the behavior of other nations. The strategies by which arms control quests are pursued will be designed to cope with the activities of other nations. These activities will be examined in later chapters which analyze the interaction stages—approach, attainment, implementation, and maintenance—by which arms control outcomes are achieved.

Although arms control may occur without being consciously sought (as when nations unconsciously observe tacit restraints), we shall examine the political determinants from the perspective of the policy maker to discover what general considerations will make a policy maker desire arms control. We will also consider what conditions in the world will generate such considerations in the policy maker's mind.

Sometimes policy is a consequence not so much of conscious rational thought as it is of processes of administrative politics. Some recent comprehensive studies of policy production on key issues of national security policy have focused upon this level.[1] Such studies center upon governmental structure and operation, group interests, and process determination rather than upon conscious rational policy making. These determinants can be important in the making of any governmental policy—even national security policy, which might be expected by virtue of its grave implications for the future of the nation to be somewhat insulated from such effects. In American arms control policy making, particularly important are the policy relations between the Department of Defense (especially International Security Affairs and the Secretary of Defense), the State Department (particularly the Arms Control and Disarmament Agency and the Secretary of State), the Joint Chiefs of Staff, and the Executive Office of the President. Congress, with the possible exception of the Joint Committee on Atomic Energy, does not generally play a significant direct political role in the formulation of arms control policy except when the Executive envisages an eventual treaty requiring Senate ratification and seeks to avoid the legendary errors of Woodrow Wilson. But if Congress itself is unlikely to produce such policy, it is nonetheless able to exercise considerable indirect influence. In recent years, this influence has been generally inhibitory due to the negative attitude toward arms control and especially disarmament shared by many Congressmen and in turn by a number of powerful Washington lobbies. Unfortunately, there is little information on how important the administrative process is in determining arms control policy. However, as scholars reconstruct the making of arms control policy, it may become possible to test propositions about the administrative political determinants of arms control policy making.

Four basic determinants merit attention in the examination of the political conditions under which a nation might be expected to be interested in arms control: personal idiosyncracies of public officials; role requirements of governmental officials; governmental structure and operation; and nongovernmental aspects of society, such as its accepted

[1]See Samuel P. Huntington, *The Common Defense* (New York: Columbia University Press, 1961); and Warner Schilling et al., *Strategy, Politics, and Defense Budgets* (New York: Columbia University Press, 1962).

values, public opinion, degree of national unity, and extent of industrialization.

First, a nation might be expected to seek or be interested in arms control if the ideology of the policy makers and policy enactors encourages it. Important features of a proposed arms control quest may be opposed because of attitudes held by some public officials. Undertaking arms control measures will, by definition, require explicit limitation of the national military effort—an idea still abhorrent to some military and civilian officials. Arguments for armament made by the military and its supporters have often appeared inadequately conscious of the instrumental nature of military force and the military establishment. But increasing intellectual appreciation of the actual interaction of military establishments in being as well as in use has accompanied the accelerating technological development of military establishments. Deterrence is now better achieved and warfare can now be better limited not only because there are more effective and controllable weapons, but also because there is a deeper and more widespread understanding of the effects of one political-military establishment upon another. Much of the increased interest in arms control has developed since World War II out of this increasing appreciation.[2] But because arms control is a recent doctrinal offshoot of disarmament and military strategy arising from realistic understanding of international politics and appreciation of the mounting threat of major war,[3] there are still those who do not appreciate the potential merit of such limitation of national military effort; thus, should they have influence, their ideological conceptions may constrict or prevent the national quest for arms control. The aversion to limitation of military effort is compounded by a failure to appreciate the fact that in international confrontation any two nations will share some objectives: from interests in mutually beneficial nonse-

[2]On the changing view of the military toward disarmament and arms control, see Jack Raymond, *Power at the Pentagon* (New York: Harper & Row, 1964), chap. 15. See also William W. Kaufmann, *The McNamara Strategy* (New York: Harper & Row, 1964).

[3]The term "Arms Control" was used in the interwar years to describe the limited disarmament undertaken in the naval agreements. See Raymond G. O'Connor, *Perilous Equilibrium: The U.S. and the London Naval Conference of 1930* (Lawrence, Kan.: University of Kansas Press, 1962), pp. 124–125; Marion W. Boggs, *Attempts to Define and Limit "Aggressive Armament" in Diplomacy and Strategy*, Vol. 16, No. 1, University of Missouri Studies (Columbia, Mo.: University of Missouri Press, 1941); and S. Yefimov, "Disarmament or the Arms Race?" *International Affairs*, February (1962), pp. 3–4.

curity trade to desires of avoiding major nuclear war. The nature of such shared interests and objectives has been examined in some applied literature on game theory,[4] although the extent of these shared objectives in international security affairs has not yet been fully determined.[5] Indeed, the lack of literature itself on this important aspect reflects the inadequate appreciation of the potential desirability of limited cooperation with an adversary. On a national scale, such attitudes, when shared by policy makers, will tend to inhibit the national quest for arms control.

Another possible inhibitor of the arms control quest is unwillingness to risk possible loss of face. Individual nature, or conditioning, has led some men to insure while others gamble. The great element of uncertainty and risk in international security agreements on alliance and arms control, which is often coupled with an inadequate understanding of the exact nature of the uncertainty and risk and a failure to compare such risks with those arising in the absence of agreement, may further inhibit the national quest.[6] Similarly, an unwillingness to risk losing face, which seems to be particularly characteristic of some civilizations as well as some individuals, may inhibit the national quest.

If limitation of the national military effort, cooperation with the adversary, or substantive risk taking are feared by policy makers or if they become unattributably manifest in the administrative process, they may serve to inhibit the quest for arms control. If these conditions are unimportant or lacking entirely, a nation may be expected to seek arms control, so long as the ideology or other disposition of policy makers does not otherwise inhibit such a quest.

Role requirements or determinants will be important in several ways. The military and industrial desire for maximal defense efforts is understandable and indeed justifiable, as long as it is not grounded in fear of limitation of military effort as such or in other personal idiosyncracies. The military is assigned the task of preparing for any con-

[4]See particularly Thomas C. Schelling, *Strategy of Conflict* (Cambridge, Mass.: Harvard University Press 1960); Anatol Rapoport, *Fights, Games and Debates* and *Strategy and Conscience* (Ann Arbor, Mich.: University of Michigan Press, 1960); and Kenneth E. Boulding, *Conflict and Defense* (New York: Harper & Row, 1962).

[5]But see Thomas C. Schelling and Morton H. Halperin, *Strategy and Arms Control* (New York: Twentieth Century, 1961); and see the discussion of the possible objectives of arms control in Chapter 1.

[6]For an analogical analysis of uncertainty and risk, see Charles J. Hitch and R. N. McKean, *Economics of Defense in the Nuclear Age* (Cambridge, Mass.: Harvard University Press, 1961), chap. 10.

tingency as best it can convince the Executive and Congress it should, and industry is consigned the possibility of seeking expanded production and profits in a Capitalist economy. But neither the military nor industry is expected—or asked—to establish political-military policy. Answers to the question whether limitations upon the military establishment are desirable depend upon answers to more fundamental questions, such as, what threats and promises are to be met, and how? In a nonmilitary government, these questions are answered by the political officials. The role requirements of officials in a nonmilitary government may not encourage them to seek arms control, but most probably they will not inhibit such seeking. Indeed, the requirements faced by most public officials who are responsible for the allocation of scarce resources as well as for national security will probably make it hard for them to formally oppose arms control. This is one reason why multinational discussion of general and complete disarmament does and probably must continue periodically.

Considerations arising from the structure and operation of the government suggest three further propositions about the quest for arms control as determined by national political considerations. First, a nation will tend to seek arms control when national policy objectives themselves suggest this quest. That is, when the objectives of the nation are such that they may be served by arms control measures (as discussed above in Chapter 1), the nation will tend to seek arms control. But this proposition must be qualified. Arms control policy will tend to be a nation's choice when the generalized and cumulated cost of the quest and maintenance expected does not outweigh the benefits expected from the arms control measure. And arms control will probably be sought when expectations of developments without arms control do not vitiate the present attractiveness of arms control.

Finally, nongovernmental considerations would be expected to intervene predominantly, if at all, in the form of public opinion exercising the anticipatory sanction of electoral or violent dissent. Thus, a nation may be expected to be interested in arms control when the attitude of the public or the polity encourages this and particularly when there is a pronounced public role in foreign policy by which public political pressures may determine the fate of officials. But such a nongovernmental effect may be vitiated if it conflicts with the attitudes or ideologies of public leaders. Thus, not surprisingly, arms control will be most sought when it is desired by both public officials and the attentive or otherwise active public.

It is difficult to verify such general propositions as those presented here because of the frequent unreliability of national statements about its policy making and its policy. Propaganda aims, popular requirements, and deceptive formulations intended to allow escape options in the event of embarrassment may distort public statements and thus one may not be able to rely on national statements. It is this weakness of political research which, above all others, limits us to development of little more than tendency statements at this time about a policy area so little investigated as arms control.

External Political Conditions

International political occurrences are obviously constituted by the actions of nations, and in some circumstances by those of other actors, such as transnational groupings and multinational organizations. These unit actions are determined or conditioned not only by the internal political and material conditions of these nations, but also by external political conditions. Thus, examination of the determinants of a nation's quest for arms control must include consideration of the same features of other nations, which become external features to the nation whose policy is under consideration. In a sense, these external political conditions constitute much of the environment in which a nation's policy makers decide and in which its diplomats and soldiers implement those decisions.

Such action takes place in what has come to be widely called "the international system." This system can be viewed as being composed of the interacting national political units (plus other units, such as the United Nations or alliances), for indeed the essence of any system is the interrelation of its constituents. An international system as here conceived can be characterized by three fundamental features: its structure, its environment (the cumulated material conditions), and its process.

Process describes a nation's, or group of nations', rules for action, such as international law, protocol, accepted procedures, and other conventions. Process determinants regulate the actions of nations and hence contribute toward the determination of the substance of their interaction. International politics is characterized more generally by disorder and change than are most national politics because there exists no strong and controlling central authority and because often the "rules of the game" are harder to create and easier to destroy in international politics than in national politics.

Political and military "rules of the game" have never been easily created in any society or system, mainly because of the absence of a central authority. The virtual impossibility of legislating, or even codifying, international law has forced greater reliance upon evolved and discovered rules—those found in "customary" behavior, international "tradition," and recognized "precedent," but not "sanctified" in accepted and observed international law. Examples are most clearly found in the *rules* (rather than the *laws*) of war. Such rules, for example, long protected civilians from attack, but became early casualties in recent wars fought with napalm and atomic bombs and indeed even conventional obliterating explosives. Such rules protected all from chemical weapons following the dread practice of World War I, but have become early casualties with civilians in prominent guerrilla warfare and counterinsurgency operations.

It appeared that such "rules of the game," mainly in the guise of shared or reciprocated restraints or limitations, were further developed in the Korean conflict[7] and in the subsequent international political maneuver to avoid direct confrontation between the major powers and to encourage abstinence in certain types of arms racing and the military exploration and exploitation of space.[8] But such rules as may have been established have suffered gravely, although not surprisingly, in asymmetrical situations where one side has compensated for another's existing advantage by breaking into a previously quarantined area of the map, of the arsenal, of the populace, or of the political practice.

The massive technological development of the postwar period has increased the ease with which such rules may be destroyed. It has served to undermine traditional distinctions and break down previously pronounced differences so that, for example, one might more easily take the first or any further escalating step because it is so "newly small."[9] And it has undermined the will to resist such rule destruction by frequently offering what may prove to be newly effective or efficient ways to combat old menaces, as in the use of chemicals to capture guerrillas. Following such rule destruction, the reacceptance of a broken rule will generally prove impossible because its strongest claim to observance lies in its not having been broken. And the creation of new

[7]See Morton H. Halperin, *Limited War in the Nuclear Age* (New York: Wiley, 1963), chap. 3.

[8]See Evan Luard (ed.), *The Cold War* (New York: Praeger, 1965), chap. 11.

[9]See Herman Kahn, *On Escalation: Metaphors and Scenarios* (New York: Praeger, 1965), for an analytical presentation of forty-four such rungs on the escalation ladder.

rules requires, above all else, a gestation that cannot be easily shortened.

These remarks should suggest the potential impact of arms control measures upon the international system. But if a nation is to seek arms control, it must first assess not only its own political and material conditions, but also those of other nations as they are manifest in their plans, means, and actions (and as these in their turn constitute the structure, environment, and process of the international system). What conditions, then, found outside the nation itself, will tend to encourage a nation to seek arms control if internal conditions do not commensurately discourage this?

The key external variables that will tend to determine a nation's interest in achieving arms control agreements with another nation or nations will be position, power, and role.

POSITION

Some product of geography and allegiance—position—will mark some nations as allies, others as adversaries, and others as uncommitted. Generally, allies are alternatives to arms control, for they may serve to compound the military establishment, particularly when technology or economy have placed effective limits upon internal development. Hence, a nation will tend to be more interested in arms control when allies are less attainable or more costly, provided that its failure to attain allies does not automatically consign them to the adversary. Thus, as the "permanent" postwar alliances disintegrate, it may be expected that the superpowers will become increasingly interested in settlements or ententes in areas of previous major confrontation like Central Europe and in areas of potential major confrontation like South Asia.

The existence of uncommitted nations may itself encourage the major nations to seek arms control agreements. A major power might encourage nonalignment not only to deprive the adversary of assistance, but also to ease the burden and risk of competitive arming. For example, both the United States and the Soviet Union seem increasingly interested in preserving the noncommitment of India not simply to maintain the configuration in South Asia, but also to allocate the financial burden of aid among both sides. One might expect similar increasing interest in insulating Africa from the cold war and perhaps, should it slip from American domination, Latin America.

The effect of allies upon pursuit of arms control will depend upon the value of the ally to the nation considering arms control. A nation will tend to choose arms control if its allies do not seriously object or if, perhaps, they insist upon it. But continued pursuit of arms control in the face of allied opposition will depend upon the importance of the allies to the nation considering arms control and upon the influence of the allies over that nation. This influence is a strange commodity, for the more power (or capacity to shape the fate) which one nation has over another, the more the dominated nation can influence the action of the powerful. An example of this is the threat to "collapse into communism" often made to the United States by weak allies. But when security considerations do not predominate, subtler, but nonetheless discomfiting, threats may be posed by dissident allies to prestige and leadership. This sort of threat is exemplified in the actions and attitudes of France toward the United States and of Communist China toward the Soviet Union in the mid-1960s. Although such allies are not essential to the security of their bloc leaders, they can loosen or jeopardize the bonds of the blocs by being successfully insubordinate.

It is important at this point to distinguish between the superpowers, whose considerations we have been examining, and the "would-be" great powers. Would-be great powers, like China and France at this time, are apt to be hostile to any arms control proposals that would not reduce the margin between them and the superpowers; these nations are in a "catch-up" position in which the development and production curves are much more favorable to them than to the more fully developed nations. As long as time and continued effort seem on their side, they are unlikely to adopt any arms control measures that would interest their superiors. There is also, however, the "has-been" great power, like Great Britain, which has recently made economic decisions terminating maintenance of greatness; a "has-been" power becomes interested in arms control measures that allow decreases in defense maintenance as well as in measures designed to keep the weak powers subjugate. Some international analysts predict a "has-been" status eventually for France (barring technological assistance from Britain and economic assistance from West Germany) and perhaps even Communist China, because of the massive leads in technology and economic capacity of the two superpowers (Russia and the United States). At that time, these nations will probably seek arrangements to make the shrinkage of their global military capabilities less obvious and less painful, as well as less expensive.

After the superpowers, the would-be great powers, and even the "has-been" powers, there are the weak powers. The military spheres of these nations are generally local, and their efforts and concerns are directed at comparable neighbors. However, the subsystems which these local interests and activities create become a major international political problem, for they tend to be characterized by local arms races and conflicts. These races and conflicts would probably not be gravely dangerous beyond their borders were the superpowers and the would-be powers not so apt to find themselves serving as external inputs into the subsystems. However, even if the local governments were not interested in arms control measures (such as arms embargoes and weapon-free zones), the major powers could undertake control measures, in effect "closing" the local political subsystems by ceasing to function as external variables. But such control measures could be undertaken only if the major powers were satisfied of the reliability of the agreement reached and could accept the local alignment consequences of their inaction.

POWER

The second key unit variable, power, raises considerations of means and, especially, of armament. This variable is itself one determinant of position in that it sets limits: The technological and applied armament capabilities and the economic strength underlying them determine the possibility that a previously weak nation may become stronger, or a previously would-be power may become a superpower. Realizing this, a nation will be more interested in achieving arms control measures that slow the development of less powerful ascendant adversaries and, conversely, will be less inclined to accept arms control proposals from nations superior to it, unless in each case the thresholds between significant power-position levels are apparently unbreachable. Interestingly, this seems to be the case for the distinction between the two superpowers and the would-be great powers, although the would-be great powers do not yet recognize or admit it.

ROLE

But also related to the position and power variables is the third unit variable—role—which determines the plans and actions of a nation. It may be misleading to view nations as revolutionary or status quo in their general objectives, for there is no nation that would not be happier under some different circumstances and none that would not be prepared to pay some price for such desired change. But there are significant differences among nations regarding their satisfaction with the momentary international configuration and regarding their willingness to undertake alteration of it by violent or internationally illegal means. Thus, in a world of many revolutionary states one would expect considerable interest on the part of a conservative nation in arms control measures, which in general tend to impede change, particularly violent change. Similarly, one would not expect a revolutionary nation to be interested in arms control measures if it confronted a conservative array of powers.

Because the orientation of a nation will shape its plans and actions, the nation assessing the external determinants of its policy will be particularly concerned to discriminate between allies and adversaries in tailoring its policies to national roles. It has been suggested previously that if allies insist on arms control or do not seriously object to its undertaking, a nation may seek arms control. The importance of this consideration will clearly be a function of the importance of the ally to the country and of the relative power each nation has over the other.

In the case of an adversary, the nation's assessment will focus not so much upon the interests of the other nation as upon the arms control measure itself. It might be thought that agreement on arms control measures between adversaries must be impossible because of divergent national interests. But such consideration ignores limitation in war—one type of arms control that has always characterized national interaction—and the actual achievement of limited arms control measures already undertaken. How might such agreement be explained in the face of strongly divergent interests? Clearly, short-run objectives can coincide, while long-term objectives or national interests remain divergent. Just as both sides may wish to limit a war, both powers may—and will—wish to avert general nuclear war. And just as the superpowers, the has-been powers, and the weak powers agreed upon a nuclear test-ban, so might such powers concert upon a nonproliferation agreement. It is also true that agreement upon such measures may result from different objectives or different assessments of likely consequences. Indeed, the only requisite for arms control or any other multinational agreement is coincidence of instrument—agreement to undertake a measure, regardless of its actual consequences or of differing state objectives. Hence, when a nation is assessing the external unit determinants of its behavior or condition of its quest for arms control, it will be attentive to the interests of its allies and to the instruments of its adversaries, a transmutation accounted for by the substantial differences in objectives among adversaries and by the absence of a common adversary in relations among adversaries.

Systemic Determinants

A nation's attitude toward arms control will be a product not only of assessment of unit variables, but also of national consideration of international systemic determinants which are here organized around structure, environment, and process.

The structure of the system has been conceived as the product of the geographical distribution, or configuration, and the political alignment of its constituents. It has been argued that a nation's prime arms control concern with adversaries will be the possible existence of interests or objectives shared or tradable and that allies will probably be viewed as a hedge against failure of the peace or of the cooperative controlling relations entered into with adversaries. In this light, strong alliances would appear to be favorable to arms control among the major powers. And it does appear likely that a bipolar world will make more possible arms control agreements by superpowers or by lesser powers graced with alliance protection, by stable local arms situations, or perhaps by entire blocs.

However, while degeneration of alliances will make expectations unclear, it might also re-establish a situation in which nations could better afford the risk of disarmament by finding it increasingly possible to compensate for internal cutbacks and constraints through external assistance or contribution, as was characteristic of the balance-of-power system before it was curtailed by "permanent" alliances.

But if nonaligned nations may serve as contributors to the security of the parties to substantial disarmament, their primary interest for a major power and bloc leader will nonetheless continue to be as indicators of the future promise of the international order—promise of victory or threat of defeat in the long-range struggle for the "minds and hearts of men." Nations in this world where material gain is rarely possible externally have been forced to tailor their hopes as well as their expectations to the immaterial world of similarity, compatibility, and occasional allegiance in the developing states. Thus, it would be unwarranted to expect a superpower to undertake long-range disarmament commitments if it did not believe that over time the rest of the world would come its way. This is the (at least momentary) symmetrical beauty of the dominant liberal democratic and international communistic worldviews, each of which is still unshakably convinced that time (if perhaps not always every specific immediate development) is on its side. And thus, by extension, if the deterioration of alliances should proceed more rapidly in the adversary's camp, a nation would be apt to be willing to run risks in arms control because of the increased assurance it would derive from its faithful allies, but perhaps less interested in seeking arms control because more optimistic about the unfolding developments and perhaps even somewhat more fearful of preventive political and military action by a slipping rival. The uncertainty about such possible motivations suggests the desirability of examining the context in which the structural systemic determinants operate for a nation.

The primary environmental determinants to be perceived by the policymaking state will be economic, technological, and military. Economically, a nation may be inclined to intensify an arms race in order to weaken an adversary more pressed; similarly, it might expect adversaries and allies to be more interested in arms control (and hence perhaps willing to pay a higher price for such agreements) under the same conditions. It is also possible that perception of opportunities for the sale of weapons might weaken a nation's interest in pursuing arms control that would curtail local arms races elsewhere. In general, however, it seems unlikely that perceptions of external economic conditions will substantially affect a nation's attitude toward arms control unless it perceives major economic resilience advantages in adversaries that would tend to outstrip possible allied efforts. That either of the superpowers should feel this so strongly as to make what had been questions of allocation become questions of capability, seems unlikely and hence unimportant as a possible determinant.

Technological considerations, however, may prove very significant. It has been shown that developments in the technologies of destruction, transportation, and communication have forced a shift from defense to deterrence and a reliance upon indirect approaches of drift and erosion embodied in indirect strategies of posture and maneuver. This has clearly changed the functions of armament substantially in ways that may offer increased opportunities for arms control.

First of all, it is possible that attainment of a virtual technological plateau—characterized, perhaps, more by the difficulty of achieving new breakthroughs on active defense than by acceptance of the unlikelihood of novelty—may render quantitative arms control of greater possible significance. It often appears that the significance of a measure and its attainability vary inversely. If this is indeed true, one might expect a nation viewing a technological stalemate to intensify quantitative efforts to gain advantage, while at the same time to pursue qualitative restraints that would tend to institutionalize or extend the plateau.

But considerations about arms control possibilities will probably continue to focus upon the levels and nature of armament because of its potential consequences rather than because of its unprofitableness. As was suggested earlier, certain existing armaments under certain circumstances may contribute toward the coming of war by creating incentives to pre-empt, or they may facilitate, if not necessarily cause, war by mischief, inadvertence, accident, or miscalculation. Similarly, the nature of military establishments and the perception of threats may combine to encourage certain kinds of arms races which, under some circumstances, may eventuate in war; such kinds of arms races range from the development of hostility and hostile deployment, through quantitative armament, qualitative armament, and mobilization to adverse expectations and escalation of military activity. The interest of a nation in arms control will be affected not only by its perceptions of these dangers, which constitute material national determinants, but also by its perception of similar interest by adversaries and allies in averting such dangers.

If conventions such as international law and limitation procedures are dominant and the international society is characterized by law observance by participants and stability as a system, the opportunities for arms control are greater. This will be true both because arms control tends to be a static remedy for frequently dynamic ills, and because there will be more opportunity for legal regulation of armament instead of more power-political regulation. Similarly, if conventions about limitation of confrontation and violent interaction are strong, the opportunities for arms limitations through sophisticated perception and communication will be greater and, hence, will encourage the national quest for arms control. But confidence in conclusions about these determinants depends further upon examination of the stages of arms control interaction by which national actions are integrated in the approach to and the attainment, implementation, and maintenance of arms control measures.

PART II

The Determinants
of Arms Control Outcomes

CHAPTER 4

The Approach
to Arms Control

The Stages of Arms Control

The possible determinants of a nation's interest in arms control were analyzed in Part I. We now turn to a study of the stages by which national quests for arms control produce arms control outcomes. Chapter 4 will analyze the ways nations approach arms control and will concentrate upon types of negotiation. Chapter 5 will focus upon the types and aspects of international agreement by which arms control may be attained. Chapter 6 will examine the necessary and possible functions of such aspects of arms control as administration, adjudication, inspection and verification, and control in the implementation of arms control agreements. Chapter 7 will consider the contributions to the maintenance of an arms control agreement that might be made by provisions for accession, resolution, elaboration, specification, and alteration.

This analysis of the stages of arms control will be more comprehensive and more systematic than inquiries devoted to examination of a specific measure or of possible measures in a specific context. Immediate political problems and specific interests will not be a major concern, except as examples, until Part III. But we will ignore neither underlying persistent political and material reality nor the determinant role of national interests in arms control, for these conditions will be elements of international political interaction. At times, we will abstract from specific aspects and measures of arms control, but we will not overlook the functions to be played by these aspects and measures. Hence, our conclusions should be relevant to past and future national interaction and should be somewhat less subject to the obsolescence and error which almost inevitably afflict any contemporary assessment.

Our approach in these four chapters will often appear to presume that international politics and foreign policy are more manipulable than practitioners have generally granted.[1] Increasing manipulability seems to characterize two levels of interaction: strictly limited conflict and declaratory conflict. In both cases, it appears to be a product of the increasing nonmanipulability of international nuclear political activity. The wide recognition of the unacceptability of general nuclear war seems to have encouraged both limited war (in situations where fears of escalation in both participation and weaponry are slight) and general declaratory policy (such as "massive retaliation" and "limited strategic war" doctrines—particularly city-avoidance strategies).

Manipulability of the sort relevant to arms control measures is highly dependent upon bipolarity. While this world is becoming decreasingly bipolar, crucial aspects (particularly those military distinguishing the superpowers from others) persist. And even where these aspects seem likely to lessen, continued presumption of bipolarity will allow greater analytical clarity. In other words, processes such as negotiation and control can be understood and analyzed more clearly in two-party terms. Our considerations need not be complicated until we apply our conclusions to the projections and analyses of the final two chapters of this book.

Our analysis in this part will also concentrate upon more formal processes of interaction and more substantial measures of arms control as it moves from approach to attainment and then to implementation and maintenance of arms control agreements; as will be seen, the nature of these stages will be clearer if they are examined in their explicit rather than their tacit forms and because their elements (particularly inspection and control) will be more important components in more substantial arms control agreements.

The Times of Approach to Arms Control

Not only the substance, but also the methods, characteristics, and procedures by which arms control is approached will be influenced by the time and conditions in which arms control agreement is sought.

[1]See, for example, Charles Burton Marshall, *The Limits of Foreign Policy* (New York: Holt, Rinehart and Winston, Inc., 1954); and Louis J. Halle, "On Teaching International Relations," *Virginia Quarterly Review,* 40 (1964), pp. 11–25.

Most thought about arms control has presumed peacetime, and much has at least claimed to presume conditions approximately those of the contemporary cold-war period with sporadic partial *détente* (such as developed in East-West relations in 1955, 1959, and 1963). However, it may appear that many propositions—especially those devoted to substantial disarmament—presume a state, beyond *détente,* of accommodation and, indeed, some proposals—such as agreed destruction of Communist China's nuclear facilities—presume condominium.

In important senses, all such peacetime-presuming propositions are distinguishable from those presuming wartime. Nonetheless, limitation of the extent and damage of war—should it come—is a long-standing and accepted objective of peacetime arms control; and the pioneering analysis of Thomas Schelling has demonstrated how comparable the wartime "negotiation" and acceptance of tacitly agreed limits can be to some peacetime arms control. Schelling has written, "Perhaps the psychology and the sanctions and the mode of communication, the kinds of reasoning involved, the lack of formal agreement or even acknowledgment, that typify limited war, represent a more central and typical process of international negotiation than we usually give it credit for."[2] And while the similarities of wartime to peacetime arms control measures are particularly clear in obviously limited wars, such as those fought in Korea and Vietnam, all wars have been limited in some ways. Today there are increasing efforts to find limited ways of using quite unlimited large or "strategic" nuclear weapons through so-called limited strategic retaliation and some types of limited nuclear war.[3] Thus, limited war itself, beyond specific arms control measures taken before and during its conduct, can be viewed as an example of arms control, for one objective of arms control is to limit the scope and damage of military activity, whether for humanitarian or strategic reasons.

And if arms control measures can be found in wartime, they may also be found in post-wartime. Indeed, the very termination of a war will include measures of arms control, particularly constraints upon the use and probably the possession of armaments and upon militant activities, either voluntarily accepted by all parties or imposed by the

[2]Thomas C. Schelling, "Reciprocal Measures for Arms Stabilization," in D. Brennan (ed.), *Arms Control, Disarmament, and National Security* (New York: Braziller, 1961), p. 176.

[3]See, for example, Klaus Knorr and Thornton Read (eds.), *Limited Strategic War* (New York: Praeger, 1962).

winners upon the losers. Such terminal constraints following a nuclear war would almost certainly mesh quickly into post-wartime arms control measures designed to avert further conflict, a new arms race, and perhaps even alliance.[4]

Possible Approaches to Arms Control

The most obvious approach to arms control agreement is negotiation. The view of negotiation as a formal diplomatic discussion is too limited, but even in its broadest sense negotiation does not include two other important ways in which arms control may be approached:

1. *Discovery.* Discovery refers to the realization that limitations have been in effect, although not consciously recognized. This is seen most clearly in cases of limited war, where the participants realize that sanctuaries are being observed (or, at least, have not been violated), or that certain weapons are not being employed, or that certain types of warfare are not being fought. But it may also be the product of a more conscious search for conventions, habits, and salient distinctions which can be discovered and recognized and further observed to insure that the hostility and conflict remain limited.

Many of these conventions, habits, and distinctions are in fact arbitrary and casuistic. They become accepted constraints or arms control measures because they are precedented or because they are in some way salient, prominent, and easily recognized by all parties. They tend to be characterized by simplicity, uniqueness, discreteness, and susceptibility to qualitative definition. Thus, the differences between relatively clean, small tactical nuclear weapons and their conventional counterparts reside almost entirely in the minds of those people who understand the scientific bases for their operation rather than in the perceptions of those people who observe or measure their effects on the battlefield. Yet, such limited nuclear weapons are not used by any nuclear nation because of fears of escalation and recognition that there are no salient nuclear firebreaks.[5] The understood "prohibition" on the use of nuclear weapons has in a sense been "discovered" by nuclear

[4]Herman Kahn has often argued that a limited or sharply curtailed nuclear war may make possible major arms control or even world government. This is a species of the argument that arms control will be more likely to be achieved in crisis than in *détente.*

[5]See Thomas C. Schelling, *Strategy of Conflict* (Cambridge, Mass.: Harvard University Press, 1960), appendix A.

powers in their adolescence and has been subsequently reinforced by continued observance, discussion, and institutionalization in the moratorium and limited ban on nuclear testing. The most recent case is China, which upon accession to the nuclear club immediately announced that it would not be the first to use nuclear weapons.

The feature which clearly differentiates such discovery from other approaches to arms control is its independence from intercourse between opposing parties. As Morton Halperin wrote in his analysis of limited war, "The necessary condition for the stabilization of a local war is agreement within the decision system of each side—and not agreement between the two sides—that further expansion is undesirable."[6] Halperin contends that conscious decision on each side, rather than negotiation between the sides, produces and maintains most limitations. The process of discovery described here is similar to Halperin's thesis in that perception and action is unilateral, but the resulting limitation has the same effectiveness as if it had been negotiated through discussion or conscious interaction. The key element is a shared domestic decision that a limitation, which happens to be recognized, or "discovered," is desirable, rather than negotiation.

2. *Imposition.* The second basic way in which arms control measures can be approached without negotiation is imposition. Arms control measures may be achieved when by will and action the stronger party imposes them on the weaker one. Indeed, most cases of substantial disarmament have been instances of imposition following upon war. In general, the same types of provisions (administration, inspection and verification, control, and others, which will be considered in Chapters 6 and 7) will characterize imposed arms control, but the nature of these provisions will be different and their ease will be greater. To varying degrees, it is true, most international political activity involves imposition: The superpowers use their superiority to shape their relations with lesser nations, and between one another they exploit comparative advantages. Imposition can involve negotiations, as, for example, in the construction or at least the ratification of peace terms or treaties. But, in fact, most arms control measures, while shaped by comparative advantage, will nonetheless be undertaken by nations where what imposition occurs will not be sanctioned by previous unconditional surrender, and thus such measures can be considered to occur among fully sovereign states.

[6]Morton H. Halperin, *Limited War in the Nuclear Age* (New York: Wiley, 1963), p. 35.

Approaches and Measures

Arms control measures were categorized into four basic types in Chapter 1: prescribed revelation of information, prescribed military postures, proscribed allocations, and prescribed rules for action. Any of these types might be approached by negotiation, and any might be imposed by the strong upon the weak. But some arms control measures are more apt to be approached and attained by discovery than others.

Revelation of information was characteristic of national policy in the nineteenth century, even though it was a period of revolutionary developments in ordnance and naval architecture. Bernard Brodie has written that "there is no doubt that the utility of modern secrecy concerning weapons was in large measure a discovery, just as many techniques of total mobilization, including the intricate ways of war-financing that we now know, represent real administrative discoveries or inventions comparable to technological inventions."[7] This discovery and appreciation of the values of secrecy has grown and persisted in our nuclear age, but while research and development secrecy has increased, procurement and battlefield-effect secrecy appears to give way increasingly (particularly in the West) to calculated leaks and military demonstrations designed to impress upon adversaries the nature and capabilities of the military establishment and thereby to strengthen its deterrent effect. Surprise in wartime has lost much of its appeal, if not effect, as wartime itself has become increasingly unappealing. And patterns of revelation persist and are inherited by successive regimes.

To a lesser extent but in a similar fashion possible military postures and "impossible" allocations are inherited and discovered—manifest, for example, in the aversion to germ warfare and in mutual restraint in the military exploitation of outer space. However, the military exploitation of space, like biological warfare preparations, seems to be a practice that it is understood will not be pressed beyond the development stage, rather than an allocation not to be made and a posture not to be struck. Consequently, measures such as these are more usefully considered rules for action comparable to those encouraging mutual restraint in the use of nuclear weapons. All are cases of

[7]Bernard Brodie, "Military Demonstration and Disclosure of New Weapons," *World Politics*, 5 (1953), p. 288. On demonstrations, see also Alfred Vagts, *Defense and Diplomacy: The Soldier and the Conduct of Foreign Relations* (New York: King's Crown, 1956), chap. 7; and W. P. Davison, *Power—The Idea and Its Communication* (P-1869, Santa Monica, Calif.: RAND Corporation, 1959).

arms control, approached and achieved mainly through discovery and subsequently reinforced through negotiation and, occasionally, agreement.

Negotiation

There are two types of negotiation; each is differentiated by the relations of the national interests involved. When the objective is shared and cooperation is required for its attainment, efforts are made to reach agreement through *cooperation*, or coordination, *negotiation*. Peace making is an example of this type of negotiation, for it requires mutual agreement to stop shooting and accept principles of demarcation and practice. When objectives are not shared, but when each party can offer something desired by the other, each trades goods for betters, and *bargaining negotiation* has occurred. Trading prisoners of war would exemplify bargaining negotiation.[8] But regardless of the type of negotiation undertaken, certain fundamental features, apart from substance, will constitute the nature of negotiation, and variations in these features will differentiate one instance from another.

1. *Participation.* How many parties negotiate, and which ones? The basic or simplest type is bilateral negotiation. Bilateral negotiation has proved increasingly difficult to justify to excluded nations— particularly in arms negotiations, where nonaligned nations and, more so, allies, can argue that whatever might be decided by the superpowers would directly affect their interests. This consideration, coupled with the argument that the presence of "third parties" (particularly the nonaligned, but also "moderating" allies) will allow mediation and might even permit and provide additional ideas, has led to an increasing tendency to multilateral conferences on arms control. In addition, the increasing importance of the "third world" and new states as sources of effective military risks of war and of worsened relations among the major powers seems likely to encourage the further expansion of participation in the hope of attaining global agreement, despite the potential explosion of difficulties in attaining agreement and accession.

Until 1956, disarmament bodies established by the United Nations

[8]See Fred C. Ikle, *How Nations Negotiate* (New York, Harper & Row, 1964), p. 2; and Michael Lindsay, *Is Peaceful Coexistence Possible?* (East Lansing, Mich.: Michigan State University Press, 1960), p. 117.

consisted of the members of the Security Council, plus the occasional addition of Canada. The United Nations Disarmament Commission, established in 1952, was expanded from eleven to twenty-five members in 1957 and enlarged to include the full U.N. membership the following year. Meanwhile, however, the Commission in 1954 formed a subcommittee of five, which lasted until 1957 and was followed by the Testban Conference conducted by representatives of the major nuclear powers. A ten-member disarmament committee existing outside the United Nations met in 1959 and 1960 and was followed by the eighteen-nation committee established in 1961. These changes in commission were largely changes in composition, reflecting both the tendency toward inclusiveness in the large groups and the concomitant tendency toward forming smaller groups within or outside the massive bodies. Thus, the only progress to result from the eighteen-nation committee (or more accurately seventeen, for France has always refused to participate) has been a product of the "meeting of the cochairmen"—as was the hotline—or of the three-nation Subcommittee on a Treaty for the Discontinuance of Nuclear Weapons Tests—as was the limited nuclear testban treaty. It continues to be the case that progress is not a product of the large disarmament bodies. Their justification at a time when the objective is still superpower agreement is in placation and perhaps education of "Nth nations" and in the possibility that these nations will make small contributions of mediation and ideas. Their justification will increasingly be the desire for inclusive agreements directed at the developing and unstable new states—inclusive agreements, perhaps like the testban treaty, finally arrived at by a subcommittee of superpowers and then acceded to by the lesser powers that have variously participated in large-scale preliminary consideration.

2. *Channels.* This is the second differentiating feature of negotiation. Normally, arms control negotiations are undertaken by special diplomatic representatives. But other channels, from heads of government at summit conferences to resident regular diplomats, have been and may be used. And less formal contacts, which are not official and so are not binding and perhaps because of this have sometimes proved more productive of understanding and of possibilities, take place occasionally. The best example is the ongoing series of "Pugwash" meetings attended by scientists and academicians from many nations.[9] Another

[9]Over the years, many articles on and products of the Pugwash Movement, or Conference on Science and World Affairs, have appeared in the *Bulletin of the Atomic Scientists.* The movement and the role of scientists are discussed in Robert Gilpin, *American Scientists and Nuclear Weapons Policy* (Princeton, N. J.: Princeton University Press, 1962).

channel (likely to become more important should progress be made on substantial arms control among the major powers) is the only direct diplomatic contact between the United States and Communist China: meetings which have taken place in Warsaw, every month or two for about a decade, between the nations' ambassadors to Poland. It is said that arms control issues have been among those discussed, but there is no evidence of progress.[10]

3. *Publicity.* The channels of negotiation are one determinant of the publicity of negotiations. If negotiations are covert, often the negotiation itself, to say nothing of its substance, is unknown to the public and perhaps even to most of the government. (For example, it is widely believed, but unconfirmed, that the United States raised, in covert discussions with the Soviet Union, the possibility of destruction of Communist Chinese nuclear test facilities in the autumn of 1964 when the first Chinese nuclear test was expected.) Conversely, negotiations may be open, or public, their sessions may themselves be open to the press or transcripts may become available afterwards. Such was the case with many sessions of the continuing postwar negotiations for general disarmament. More often, however, negotiations are secret, closed, or private—the fact is known, but the substance is not; transcripts are classified, although the substance or "progress" is sometimes later revealed. Such has been the case with the Eighteen-Nation Disarmament Conference, which first met in 1962.

Open negotiation is a twentieth-century development much lamented by traditional diplomatists.[11] There is indeed little reason to expect serious negotiation and substantive gain in open negotiations, both because the temptation to appeal to the various grandstands is immense and even more because the subject under negotiation— national security affairs—is so important and its private parts are so necessarily wrapped in secrecy. What explicit arms control agreements are known to have been achieved in the postwar period—notably the Antarctica treaty, the testban treaty, and the hotline agreement—have resulted from closed negotiations. It cannot be known to what extent such closed negotiations, coupled perhaps with covert negotiations, have contributed to less formal and probably unwritten arms control agreements or understandings of the sort which will be examined shortly. It seems likely that reliance on such understandings has in-

[10]Little has thus far been published about these meetings. See Richard Starnes, " 'Twilight' talks between U.S. and Red China are frail, polite—and occasionally fruitful," *Houston Chronicle,* Feb. 24 (1965).

[11]See Harold Nicolson's books, *Diplomacy* and *Evolution of Diplomatic Method* (London: Constable, 1954), for typical critiques of open negotiations.

creased as more formal negotiations have become less promising because of the difficulty of reaching agreement openly and the obstacle of
popular opposition to secret negotiation.

4. *Language.* The fourth feature of negotiation, which differentiates the less formal instances, is language. This feature is closely
related to the fifth feature—form. The "language" of negotiation is the
means or medium by which the international intercourse is carried out.
The most common language is, of course, human speech—words spoken across a table or via cable. However, if attention is focused upon
diplomatic verbal negotiation, awareness and understanding of the
national political and material underpinnings of such discourse, which
are essential to understanding the meaning of the language,[12] will often
be obscured or neglected. Particularly in matters of military policy and
arms control, the nature and activities of national military establishments must be taken to complement the words spoken by national
representatives.

Thus, because the processes of negotiation to be considered here
are comparable, this analysis will examine not only the dialogue of
words across diplomatic tables, nor only in addition the enunciation of
pronouncements across oceans and borders, but also the dialogue of
deeds. This dialogue of deeds (or in many cases, "multilogue") is
constituted by those actions which are basically symbolic and which
serve as demonstration and those actions which are of relevant effect.

This dialogue, or multilogue, of deeds, lacking as it does formal
verbal intercourse, may have one of several divergent effects. There is
a danger that its inexplicit nature may obscure important nuances. But
elimination of the risk of verbal misunderstanding in cases where the
"language" is relevant and effective rather than symbolic and concerns
capabilities, interests and intentions, and demonstrations of self-
restraint—in all of which, "actions speak louder than words"—may
bring about greater understanding and facilitate concern about limitation of arms or activity.

Such understandings are sometimes referred to as "tacit" and
might more precisely be denoted as implicit understandings, quasi
bargains, or instances of spontaneous coordination.[13] Until archives are

---

[12]Note that the difficulty of understanding the burden of Chinese Communist
diplomatic messages seems part of the explanation of the Korean conflict. See Allen
J. Whiting, *China Crosses the Yalu* (New York: Macmillan, 1960), for an analysis.

[13]The pioneer in analyzing the phenomenon of "tacit negotiation" is, once
again, Thomas Schelling. See especially Schelling's *Strategy of Conflict* and Schelling and Halperin's *Strategy and Arms Control* (New York: Twentieth Century,

opened or revealing memoirs are written, it is never possible to be certain that what were not products of open negotiation were products of tacit, rather than of secret, negotiation. But arms control measures achieved in the postwar years that may have resulted from tacit negotiation include the nuclear test moratorium of 1958 to 1961, mutual cuts in military budgets and in fissionable materials production by the United States and the Soviet Union undertaken in 1964 and 1965, and perhaps the cutbacks in ground forces undertaken throughout the 1950s. There are, of course, many other apparent informal arms understandings that persist among the major powers, among them abstention from jamming military communications, avoidance of surreptitious underwater wars of attrition, noninterference with reconnaissance satellites, refraining from political and military assassination, and observing the "prohibition" on use of nuclear weapons in limited war.[14] Many of these international understandings were discovered rather than negotiated tacitly, while the specific agreements listed above appear to have been products of tacit negotiation. Even if a measure actually has been covertly, rather than tacitly, negotiated, if the public *thinks* it the product of tacit negotiation, it may be expected to be less enforceable and so more easily broken—and therefore, perhaps, more easily accepted and undertaken.

5. *Form*. Closely related to the language of negotiation is the form of the agreement reached. National choice of an agreement's form, particularly whether it is written or unwritten, will be determined in part by the contents of the understanding. An unwritten agreement is more apt to be acceptable if its subject is easily verifiable (such as public contribution of fissionable materials to an international agency) or intentionally renouncible (such as a nuclear test moratorium). Formality will also depend upon language: A tacitly negotiated agreement will necessarily be unwritten, or at most "written" as mutual unilateral pronouncements. The many forms of agreement—from formal treaties and signed executive agreements through explicit but informal arrangements to tacit understandings—will be discussed in Chapter 5. The degrees of specificity and ambiguity are not simply determined by the written or unwritten nature of the agreement. Thus,

---

1961). A relevant and stimulating recent analysis is Charles E. Lindblom's *Intelligence of Democracy: Decision Making through Mutual Adjustment* (New York: Free Press, 1965).

[14]See Thomas C. Schelling, "Reciprocal Measures for Arms Stabilization," pp. 174–175.

a written agreement not to aggress can be much more ambiguous than an unwritten agreement not to test nuclear weapons. The nature and uses of such specificity and ambiguity will be considered in Chapter 7.

These five features of negotiation—participation, channels, publicity, language, and form—include the primary nonsubstantive differences among international arms negotiations. From the preceding analysis it should be clear that the substance of the negotiations will influence determination of some of these features and that some features may contribute to determination of the substance of negotiations. And the outcome of negotiation will depend upon the interaction of national preferences in the negotiation process.

The Negotiation Process

However negotiations may differ in features, all will share certain aspects, procedures, or stages. Schematically, the approach to agreement can be seen as beginning with unilateral decision and initiatory communication, followed by responsive perception and effect, which may bring about an interactive process terminating in an agreement decision.

The initial decision by a nation is in two analytically separable, but often interdependent, parts. The first part is the decision that negotiation is desirable. The nation deciding to undertake or to attempt to induce negotiation will probably be interested in exchanging views on substantive or procedural matters, in resolving differences through barter, or in concluding an agreement to cooperate in the attainment of shared objectives.[15] But the nation may decide to negotiate for what might be termed "side effects," such as maintaining contact with an adversary, substituting negotiation for violent action, educating the propaganda gains, or having an impact upon third parties.[16] If these objectives under the circumstances could be as easily attained by other means than negotiation, the decision to negotiate probably reflects a preference for the expected negotiated outcome to a take-it-or-leave-it consequence of unnegotiated agreement.

The infrequency with which formal arms control negotiations have resulted in agreement strongly suggests that major nations generally

---

[15]See the general discussion of some objectives of negotiation in Fred C. Ikle, *How Nations Negotiate,* chap. 3.

[16]Fred C. Ikle discussed some of these "side effects" in *How Nations Negotiate,* chap. 4.

undertake such negotiations for their side effects. It is often contended that the United States only negotiates about "general and complete disarmament" at Geneva because of the propaganda importance of matching Soviet public ardor in espousing this cause.[17] There have been, however, and there continued to be other reasons for holding such negotiations. The continued contact resulting from such disarmament sessions has allowed the breaking down of the plenary body into small working groups that were able to produce agreements on the limited testban and the hotline when political decisions within the significant countries permitted. Also, negotiations termed "technical" (stemming, in effect, from Eisenhower's "open skies" proposal in 1955) and devoted to the danger of surprise attack, as well as lengthy sessions on the detection of nuclear tests, have quite clearly served to educate both sides to the dangers and complexities previously overlooked or unregarded in public postures on disarmament.

But the side-effect benefits of negotiation are not limited to propaganda, education, and contact which would permit agreement under appropriate political conditions. For even when agreement is achieved, if that agreement is as constrained as were the limited testban and the hotline, the primary benefit may be the effect upon the tenor of relations among the major powers, embodied in concert and *détente*.

This effect and its consequences may be seen quite clearly in postwar political developments. Diplomatic negotiations became and remained inflexible and unprofitable as the cold war heightened animosities and intensified boundaries. With diplomacy thus frozen, armament was the only clearly dynamic element in the construction and posturing that has constituted most postwar international politics. Until alignments began to soften, as Communist China and Gaullist France developed infant nuclear establishments and sought opportunities to parlay them into major political instruments, arms control negotiations were virtually the only place in which political mobility and gain could be achieved through side-effect benefits, such as propaganda and education.

Increasingly, as alignments have shifted and bipolarity has been eroded, the incentives that brought the superpowers to use disarmament negotiations as occasions for bargaining and maneuvering have tended to give way to shared interests in cooperating to strengthen alignments and bipolarity by limiting the scope and freedom of "inde-

[17]See particularly John W. Spanier and Joseph L. Nogee, *The Politics of Disarmament: A Study in Soviet-American Gamesmanship* (New York: Praeger, 1962).

pendent" military establishments and re-establishing similar dependen-
cy relations among allies. Beyond technology, this is the primary reason
why attention to surprise attack and bilateral arms reductions has
tended to give way to efforts to curtail nuclear proliferation: first by
bans on nuclear testing, then by agreements not to disseminate "tested"
nuclear weapons and information, and probably later by agreements
not to disseminate delivery vehicles. It is an irony of arms control
negotiations that those times in which the superpowers could agree to
mutual reductions and with some success bring their allies to comply
were characterized by each's exploitation of side-effect benefits at the
expense of the other's alliance. This shortsighted activity further encouraged the lesser powers to undertake independent military development, which has increased the shared interests of each superpower in
arms controls but has decreased both the attainability of such controls
and either side's incentives to use arms control negotiations rather than
renewing flexible diplomatic channels and techniques to regain both
that mastery of its alliance and that auspicious interbloc posture with
which each superpower entered the cold war.

At no time in the postwar period has formal negotiation on
security affairs been a common or long-lasting occurrence. Regardless
of their specific substance, arms control and related negotiations differ
considerably from economic and from most political negotiations and
are less frequently undertaken seriously for several reasons. First, they
concern what are generally believed to be the instruments and activities
that are the essence of national security, or at least the last resort of
security. Thus, beyond the fears of impingements on valued secrecy,
nations are more wary and distrustful of formal negotiation where the
costs of failure and particularly of deception could be so far reaching
and final. Second, arms control negotiations are dealings with adversaries. Most international negotiations deal usually with friends if they
are military or political; with friends and the nonaligned if they are
economic; or with defeated nations, which cannot pose grave threats to
national security. Dealing with adversaries is apt to be politically less
acceptable to both the populace and the allies, as was suggested in
Chapter 3. Thus, nations will be less inclined to seek such agreements.
And third, arms control negotiations almost always expose and even
create many difficult technical problems.

But if it is the appreciated potential significance and consequence
of negotiations on security affairs that make serious formal negotiations
difficult, it is also that same significance and consequence that make
tacit negotiation and understanding an important part of international

political and military relations. Thus, the second aspect of the decision to initiate or undertake negotiation is of particular importance. This is the decision about the substance and nature of negotiation. If the desire is for more than side effects, the substance will be either the arms control provisions sought or the negotiation itself, which could even be viewed as an arms control measure if it served to delay military activity or to educate the participants about each other and about the dangers faced. The decision about the nature of negotiations involves selection among the five features of negotiation examined earlier—participation, channels, publicity, language, and form—and so will be informed by considerations of the likely relations among features, substance, and outcomes suggested above.

At this point begins the process tending toward agreement or realization of its unattainability. There are two distinct rounds, one initiated with proposals *of* negotiation (that is, proposals that negotiation be undertaken) and the other with proposals *for* negotiation. Proposals *of* negotiation may take many forms, but fundamentally, when not simply appeals to reasonableness ("Come, let us reason together"), they will employ argument ("It's in your interest as well as mine"), threat ("If you do not talk, I will use force"), promise ("If you will talk, I shall befriend you"), and perhaps occasionally compulsion. Such proposals of negotiation need not be made by diplomatic exchange. Particularly if the negotiation envisaged is to be tacit, the proposition may be made by pronouncement or by deed. Therefore, while proposals of testban negotiations include explicit calls for conference and appeals to common interests, proposals of defense budget cuts are generally pronouncements of unilateral intentions embellished by encouragement of replication.

The important consideration is, of course, that the proposition be received and understood—that it be communicated. There may be difficulty in assessing sincerity in explicit statements, and there may be even greater difficulty in perceiving and recognizing propositions by deed and perhaps even by pronouncement. And if, as is often the case in international politics, the message is intended for more than one nation—for all nuclear powers or for members of a major military alliance, for example —then it must be spoken so that it can be understood by all parties to which it is directed.

Once a party has perceived and recognized the proposals for negotiation, it must in turn decide upon its consequent action. It may respond by word, pronouncement, or deed; or it may publicly ignore the proposal. At this stage, ignoring a proposal is, of course, itself a responsive action, although it may not be perceived as such unless the instigator has somehow learned that the recipient did, in fact, recognize its proposal. In practice, the course of the respondent is not nearly so clear, for it must first recognize the instigation among the many other words, pronouncements, and deeds, most or all of which are inadvertent or insignificant. And further, it must select among various possible instigations, for it is likely to be receiving proposals from other nations, as well as instructions from its own interests and media. Selection between competing instigations is a primary task of a nation's political-military organs.

A nation may respond to a proposal of negotiation by accepting or rejecting it; or it may seek to modify the proposed terms of that negotiation. There may then follow further rounds of response, perception, decision, and response directed toward agreement upon the nature and terms of negotiation. But at some point, these terms will become settled enough that the content of intercourse will shift from form to substance. Then initiation will take the form of a substantive proposal, and response will take the form of agreement or counterproposal by word, pronouncement, deed, or inaction. This negotiation process described here in abstract terms is quite clear when it occurs in formal diplomatic negotiation and, indeed, in any verbal negotiation. But its manifestation in tacit negotiation is not generally so clear.

Tacit Negotiation

It is unfortunate that the conduct of tacit negotiation cannot be satisfactorily documented without research in the archives of participating nations to uncover the purposes and patterns of each party's activities. Fragmentary historical examples of tacit negotiation might include the termination of arms races and the conduct of war. But the most likely cases, such as the American-Soviet agreement upon a nuclear test moratorium and then upon cuts in defense budgets, are too recent and difficult to reconstruct. There have been, however, past cases in which strategic thought, rather than military establishment, has been clearly affected by the actions and pronouncements of adversaries. There are various examples in the development of airpower doctrine.[18] But perhaps the most revealing recent case has been the development of Soviet strategic thought in relation to that of the United States on military problems and even arms control.

[18]See George Quester, *Deterrence Before Hiroshima* (New York: Wiley, 1966).

Even by the 1960s, many American officials and analysts feared that the Soviets were too unsophisticated to appreciate, let alone respond to, the increasingly complex and creative American doctrines of deterrence and arms control. But soon, Soviet understanding became more obvious in the reactions to and reviews of American strategic literature in Soviet military journals and the more popular monthly, *International Affairs*. In autumn 1962, the Soviets published a book, *Military Strategy*, prepared by a group of officers under the supervision of Marshal V. D. Sokolovskii. Among other perceived failings, the book made slight reference to arms control and denigrated Western concepts of limited war. It was immediately translated and soon published in America and aroused what might be characterized as a reaction of despair mixed with condescending hostility on the part of many Western defense analysts. Apparently, the Soviets were surprised and troubled by this reaction, for there soon appeared a revised edition more impressive in its sophistication and less dogmatic in its treatment of limited war and arms control. Apparently, Soviet strategists had learned not only from reading and talking with American strategists, but also from noting their reaction to the Soviet production.[19]

Tacit negotiation originates when a proposal is communicated in action by an instigator to a recipient. At this stage, it is a unilateral initiative. There are two basic types of unilateral initiative: those that are self-contained or self-completing and those that are intended to be reciprocation-inducing. Hardening of a nation's missiles is a self-contained unilateral initiative, for its primary purpose as an arms control measure is achieved without reciprocation; it protects a nation's missile force so that it can withstand attack and then respond if response is desired, thus increasing national control over military capabilities. Announcing cessation of nuclear weapons tests is an initiative

---

[19]This interesting episode in the American-Soviet strategic dialogue and the Soviet doctrine manifest in it are presented and analyzed by Thomas W. Wolfe in *Soviet Strategy at the Crossroads* (Cambridge, Mass.: Harvard University Press, 1964). Thomas Schelling draws from this experience the interesting lesson that one might better influence an adversary by obviously listening to him than by speaking to him (see Schelling, "Signals and Feedback in the Arms Dialogue," *Bulletin of the Atomic Scientists,* January [1965], pp. 5–10). The best English translations of the first edition of Sokolovskii's *Soviet Military Strategy* (Englewood Cliffs, N. J.: Prentice-Hall, 1963) is that produced by RAND and edited by H. S. Dinerstein, Leon Gouré, and Thomas Wolfe. The second edition has not been published in English, but a comparison-by-quotation of the two editions, entitled *Military Strategy,* was issued by the Joint Publications Research Service of the U.S. Department of Commerce in 1963. See also Leon Gouré, "Notes on the Second Edition of Marshal V. D. Sokolovskii's *Military Strategy,*" (RM-3972-PR, Santa Monica, Calif.: RAND Corporation, 1964).

intended to induce reciprocation, probably through a combination of the impact of marshalled opinion and the increased "freedom" to undertake comparable self-limitation which a nation would feel once the other had done so. Measures that take more general form, such as announcements of cuts in military budgets, are also arms control initiatives. They are less easily categorized, for they are somewhat self-contained (in that the nation employing the cutback enjoys economic increments) and somewhat reciprocation-inducing (in that they make comparable activity by adversaries more easily justified, if not necessarily more attractive). But they also are probably intended to have a strong pedagogical impact, for they can be viewed as having been designed to instruct the adversary about his own and shared interests, to tell or remind him that he too could profit from decreased military spending.

However, the concept of initiatives in foreign policy may be in danger of losing substance. Aides of President Johnson were reported to observe that the President's 1965 State of the Union message, which raised the possibility of Soviet visits to the United States and joint Russian-American efforts to cope with the population explosion, "had been intended to set in motion 'initiatives without proposals.' "[20] The significant feature of initiatives is that they be actions or commitments undertaken unilaterally.

Psychologist Charles E. Osgood, one of the early proponents of programs of unilateral initiatives, has expressed a major reason for adoption of such policies:

Negotiated agreements require commitments from both sides prior to any action by either, and under the conditions of cold war thinking commitments of any significance seem most unlikely; as long as both sides remain chained to the requirement of prior commitment from the other, neither is able to take the initiative in moving toward a more peaceful world.[21]

Osgood describes his own program, Graduated Reciprocation In Tension-reduction (GRIT), as a reverse analogue of an arms race: "It is perhaps best viewed as a kind of international (rather than interpersonal) communicating and learning situation, where the communication is more by deeds than by words and where what is learned—hopefully and gradually—is increased mutual understanding and trust."[22] While Osgood is more optimistic about the possible effects of GRIT than some

[20]Tom Wicker, "The Johnson Message," *The New York Times,* Jan. 6 (1965).
[21]Charles E. Osgood, *An Alternative to War or Surrender* (Urbana, Ill.: University of Illinois Press, 1962), p. 84.
[22]Charles E. Osgood, *An Alternative to War or Surrender,* p. 88.

other analysts,[23] he does make the important point that initiatives must not compromise the essential military capabilities of the nation, but instead must be specific activities calculated to reduce and control international tensions and undertaken regardless of the attitude and activity of the adversaries. Only if their undertaking is unconditional (although not necessarily irreversible in time) might they serve to break the deadlock in which neither side will make the first move toward an objective that it believes to be in the interests of both. There are, of course, many problems of design and presentation raised by such a proposed program, particularly if the program is to be comprehensive rather than fragmentary and even more so if it is to induce reciprocation by several heterogeneous states. However, such a program will be based upon the same principles and psychological-political approach as those cold-war initiatives that have been undertaken, such as the nuclear test moratorium, cutbacks in production of fissionable materials, and reductions in military budgets—most of which have been reciprocated. Thus, such unilateral initiatives can be seen to represent time-honored and success-proven principles of military policy, adapted often to the service of broader political goals of tension-control and cooperation, employing the technique of tacit negotiation.

Inducing Reciprocation

The ways and means of inducing reciprocation, like those of inducing negotiation itself, have not been carefully studied. It might be suspected that inducing negotiation would be easier than inducing reciprocal substantive action, because negotiation neither implies nor entails commitment to action. Yet nations act as if they have particular aversion to negotiation, preferring other diplomatic and internal military activity. The only area in which this is not the rule is the major limitation of armaments; in this area alone, negotiations have proved, and are clearly understood to be, least likely to deal seriously with grave problems. Thus, activity has shifted to tacit negotiation.

Reciprocation might be induced by making inaction or unresponsiveness unreasonable, less desirable, more difficult, or impossible. Provision of reasons, a rather educative activity, tends to work better with friends than with adversaries. Offering goods to make unresponsiveness less desirable is quite frequent; one can view "wheat deals" as a manifestation of this behavior. The use of force is perhaps infre-

<hr>

[23]See, for example, Robert A. Levine, "Unilateral Initiatives: A Cynic's View," *Bulletin of the Atomic Scientists,* 19 (1963), pp. 22–25.

quent, but its demonstration and threat are not. It is true, as **Alfred Vagts** has written, that "most of the traditional effect of a demonstration is gone, together with the older state system among whose long-standing fictions was once the belief that the demonstrating Power was nearing the end of its patience and was contemplating serious measures. The Soviets declined to share this view, or fiction."[24] As was suggested earlier, current demonstrations in their appearance and impact increasingly resemble May Day in Moscow. And their effectiveness, with the breakdown of their symbolic nature, has been further diluted by the high degree of ambiguity resulting from the inexplicit nature of the national intentions underlying them.

Employment of threats and promises, of rewards and punishments, thus becomes very important, and it is important to have a better appreciation of the importance of one's "bargaining assets." Nonvital economic, political, and military possessions and activities (such as the American embargo on the shipment of "strategic materials" to the Soviet Union and its satellites, the retention of SAC and Polaris bases around the globe, and restrictions on economic credits) are likely to serve as tools of inducement. Compliance seems to be a function of the percipient's assessment or appreciation of the instigator, assessment or valuation of the action suggested, and prior commitments or promises. But, particularly in a time of cold war, calculation, even of the subjective sort implied in such a list of determinants, may be unlikely. Openness to signals, inquiries, propositions, requests, and proposals is likely to be determined by such traits as authority, authoritativeness, prejudice, friendship, trustworthiness, and individual idiosyncracy. There is no clear way to assess the role of each factor—much less to suggest ways of capitalizing upon them.

Nonetheless, in the era of the cold war, inducing replication if not always reciprocation—a comparable if not necessarily complementary action—may not require the study and cunning that this analysis might imply. In the arms race (as well as in the other military "races" of suspicion, deployment, mobilization, expectation, and escalation), there are usually clear tendencies for one side to respond to the other's innovations and activities with similar innovations and activities.

A recent study by Jan Triska and David Finley[25] applied to cold-war intercourse a theorem on the evolution of extended conflicts

---

[24] Alfred Vagts, *Defense and Diplomacy: The Soldier and the Conduct of Foreign Relations* (New York: King's Crown, 1956), p. 259.

[25] Jan P. Triska and David D. Finley, "Soviet-American Relations: A Multiple-Symmetry Model," *Journal of Conflict Resolution,* 9 (1965), pp. 37–53.

proposed by the Belgian sociologist Eugene Dupréel: "While the character of aggressor and defender intermingle and merge, the opposing forces tend to balance each other. They take the same forms to meet and neutralize each other more completely."[26] If this theorem holds true in areas outside of the arms race, "any stimulus inserted into a process by one of the opponents may be expected to bring about a proportionate response in kind from the other."[27] Triska and Finley's study of other areas, such as types of diplomacy, education, competition for the allegiance of the uncommitted, information and propaganda agencies abroad, and scientific research, indicates that in order to reachieve equilibrium in the system, such a proportionate response in kind is required. They conclude that beyond meeting the military challenge in kind and degree, "the United States ought to change the ground rules of the conflict by supplying new stimuli and thus opening new dimensions."[28]

If such tendencies toward replication are actual and necessary features of the cold war, perhaps the inducement of reciprocation on arms control measures will require more example setting than encouragement of comparable action by argument, goods, or force. But the impact of the deterioration of alliances and their strict bipolar world power structure upon such a tendency toward replication by a major adversary, let alone a divergent minor power, may seriously limit opportunities for tacitly negotiated reciprocal arms controls in the future. The attainment of such fundamentally bilateral control agreements may increasingly become a luxury that each party can afford only so long as its military establishment is significantly superior to the combined strength of its divergent allies and whatever satellites they have managed to obtain among the "uncommitted."

Continual Decision in Negotiation

What may begin as a unilateral initiative at the communication stage will have a unilateral effect at the intercourse or conversation stage, where it effects a decision and elicits a response, whatever the means,

---

[26]Eugene Dupréel, *Sociologie Generale* (Paris: Presses Univ. de France, 1948), p. 151; quoted in Jan P. Triska and David D. Finley, "Soviet-American Relations: A Multiple-Symmetry Model," p. 37.

[27]Jan P. Triska and David D. Finley, "Soviet-American Relations: A Multiple-Symmetry Model," p. 38.

[28]Jan P. Triska and David D. Finley, "Soviet-American Relations: A Multiple-Symmetry Model," p. 51.

and thereupon becomes a bilateral activity. Such negotiation, whether explicit or tacit, involves continuous decision, affected by shifting considerations of objectives, and criteria for success, concerning both process and substance.

As Fred Ikle has written, throughout the negotiating process nations have a "continual threefold choice": choose the available terms, choose no-agreement, or continue bargaining in an effort to improve the available terms.[29] The decision to continue negotiating rests on the belief that better terms can be obtained, although in fact the terms may get worse. For example, the Soviet Union, negotiating with Finland in the winter of 1939 to 1940, warned that if its first terms were not accepted new demands would be added; new demands were added, and the Finns felt compelled to accept these new demands before they were made even worse.[30] But a nation may prefer to run this risk, and it may find the prospect of no-agreement acceptable enough to merit running such a risk by rejecting the available terms. Presumably, this was the case in nuclear testban negotiations, until the late spring of 1963 when each side began to value agreement more than insistance on preferred terms.

In arms control negotiations, the decision to continue negotiating rather than to accept the available terms or to break off negotiations is probably often the result of an appreciation of various side effects of negotiation, many of which might not be side effects of agreement. Possible side effects of arms control negotiations might include maintaining contact, substituting negotiation for violence, gathering intelligence, educating the adversary, deceiving the adversary, making propaganda gains, and exploiting the impact upon third parties whether allied or unaligned.

A nation may choose to reject available terms and terminate negotiation because there was no consonance; but this decision may be also the result of failure to realize that consonance existed, a possibility that again emphasizes the importance of understanding among negotiators, whether it be by verbal communication or by a dialogue of deeds. Lack of agreement may vary in degree. In some cases, nonagreement may be the result of inadequate negotiation or inadequate appreciation of differences and of grounds for possible compromise. In others, no amount of analysis, reason, and acceptable compromise could produce agreement. However, even in cases of insurmountable disagreement,

[29]Fred C. Ikle, *How Nations Negotiate,* chap. 5.
[30]This incident is related in Fred C. Ikle, *How Nations Negotiate,* chap. 11.

negotiation may play a useful role. Even despite lack of agreement, the participants will have gained not only additional information about the adversary (his position and his style), but, more important, experience in negotiating. Negotiation, even more than other aspects of international political life, is both a learning process and a learned capability—particularly when it is tacit, and there is so much to be learned.

In addition, there may be propaganda benefits arising from disagreement, if the blame for failure can be sloughed onto the adversary; and there may be posture benefits if firmness and even belligerence affects the adversary. Presumably Khrushchev's brash behavior in his Vienna session with Kennedy was intended to achieve such advantageous consequences of belligerence and confidence. Interestingly, it had precisely the opposite effect upon Kennedy, convincing him that his adversary was dangerous and badly in need of firm opposition. The Cuban missile crisis and its tacit and explicit bargaining can be viewed as a product of the disagreement that characterized the negotiation at that Vienna meeting.

In an important sense, of course, negotiation never ends. When nations are not talking to each other, they are talking at each other and acting with and against each other. International intercourse can be viewed as a continuous negotiation characterized by periodic discussions. The outcomes of negotiation, momentary or lasting, are various: from changes in national objectives and commitments through clarification of points of disagreement to tacit understandings and explicit agreement. The ways in which such understandings and agreements are approached may have important effects upon the agreements attained.

CHAPTER 5

The Attainment
of Arms Control

If approaches to arms control are to culminate in attainment of arms control, interaction must uncover or create and then express international agreement. In substance, an international arms control agreement will resemble other international agreements in many ways. Much of this substance will be explicit and therefore obvious, particularly the provisions for arms control and provisions for acceptance of the agreement. But other aspects of this substance will be implicit and yet quite important, especially the underlying requirements, direction, and form of the agreement. An understanding of both the implicit and the explicit aspects of international agreement will contribute not only to the analysis, but also to the imagination, creation, and design of specific arms control measures; such understanding may therefore aid efforts to attain and maintain arms control.

The Nature of an International Agreement

Given the many conflicting long-term interests and discordant short-term objectives, international agreement might appear to be as remarkable as it seems infrequent. However, international agreement requires agreement only on the instruments with which existing and even conflicting objectives are to be sought. There are various ways of distinguishing the general objectives of an international agreement. Fred Ikle has suggested that the possible objectives of international agreements may be viewed as including extension, normalization, redistribution, and innovation, as well as side effects.[1]

[1]Fred C. Ikle, *How Nations Negotiate* (New York: Harper & Row, 1964), chap. 3.

Extension of present conditions or arrangements will require that change be controlled in some way so that the forces and developments characterizing the order over time are contained. Arms control agreements qualifying as extension agreements would include nonaggression pacts, arms embargoes, and nuclear nonproliferation agreements, as well as nuclear testbans. Although normalization agreements as such are not likely to include arms control measures, both normalization and redistribution could be viewed as possible features of agreements designed to improve upon a present world incrementally rather than systemically. Most national efforts and most international agreements probably fall within this category. Certainly, this would apply to most limited arms control measures, from creation of a hotline to agreements upon mutual finite deterrence postures.

The grave failing of many proposals is their emphasis upon the present and their inadequate recognition that the international order is constantly changing. These changes must be anticipated and provided for whenever possible, if the agreements are not to break down from obsolescence alone. This realization might suggest that all international agreements deal with a future rather than a present world. Nonetheless, there is a useful distinction to be made between those agreements that seek to work within most of the characteristic boundaries of the present developing international order and those that seek to create a different world. It may be difficult to decide whether a territorial arms control agreement in Europe should be considered a meliorative measure or an innovative measure. The answer would depend partially upon the nature and extent of the agreement's provisions and upon the emphasis the analyst places upon the political effects of substantial changes in Europe in terms of his beliefs about the nature of the international system. There would be no dispute, however, over the contention that a "general and comprehensive disarmament" agreement would be an effort to create a different future world. Indeed, this is perhaps its greatest recommendation in the minds of many of its supporters.

Creation of a different future world, it is sometimes argued, might be initiated, if perhaps not fully achieved, by the very fact of *an* agreement, which would destroy precedents of conflict and irreconcilability and at the same time create precedents of agreement and cooperative resolution of undesirable conflict. And, as was suggested in Chapter 4, the creative value of an agreement may reside in not only the side effects upon international relations and order, but also the side effects upon the adversary-partner (learning or diversion) or upon oneself (learning or productive respite). It seems more likely, however, that such creation of a new future world would result from the fact of *the* agreement—the specific provisions of the agreement—although the effects of precedent destruction and creation are important and so must be taken into analytical account.

The form of an international agreement will be greatly dependent upon the way in which it was approached. Tacit negotiation will clearly produce a tacit agreement. The traditional distinctions within the realm of the explicit agreement concern the degree of formality of the statement of agreement. Although treaties could legally be verbal, they are always written, as was the limited nuclear testban treaty. Less formal, and therefore in fact if not in law more easily broken, are mutual declarations.

The nuclear test moratorium was a product of conditional declarations. The Soviet Union terminated a test series and announced on March 31, 1958, that it would cease testing if other powers would also abstain. On August 22, the United States announced that it would suspend nuclear tests for at least a year when its testing series was completed on October 31. The Soviet Union resumed testing September 30 in retaliation for American and British tests and ended its series November 3. Although the United States announced on December 29, 1959, that it would not renew the moratorium, no tests took place and the Geneva Conference on the Discontinuance of Nuclear Weapons Tests continued until the Soviets announced on August 30, 1961, that they were resuming atmospheric testing. The unpoliced declaratory moratorium had lasted for three years but was finally terminated with relative ease.

Still less formal and generally less public are unwritten agreements of the sort which resulted in mutual American-Soviet reductions in defense budgets for fiscal 1965. The Johnson administration announced its intention to cut the defense budget by about one billion dollars, mainly by eliminating obsolescent weapons systems, dismantling unneeded bases and installations, and improving management efficiency. Shortly thereafter, the Soviets noted this announcement in revealing a similar reduction in their military budget. The significance of such reductions is unclear: Appropriations can be easily hidden elsewhere; more important, they are so informal as to be easily broken, covertly as well as openly, without obvious ill effect (as the American reduction pledge was in spirit by the subsequent supplemental defense appropriation intended largely for the war in Vietnam).

There are several senses in which an international agreement will be significant beyond its actual substance. First, it is a record, expressed in actions, in words, on paper, and perhaps even in institutions. Even a declaration will persist unless destroyed or permuted and will thus continue to be a factor in international relations. With records of its negotiation and its context, an agreement, whatever its form, is a potential source of clarification or confusion should dispute or even simple uncertainty about its provisions arise during its lifetime. This is more likely to be true of major arms control agreement than of other international political agreements, if only because it will always prove impossible, and possibly undesirable, to detail and specify all behavioral and institutional provisions to be in effect during the duration of the agreement.

More generally, an international agreement is a statement of the desire to order objectives, relations, and actions in some sphere and thereby to make the future less uncertain and presumably more favorable. That such desire is clear and expressed will influence national policy makers. Further influencing international relations will be the fact that an agreement is also a statement of the good word and good faith of the signatories. Although nations are known to break their word in many circumstances and are even expected to in some, no nation can do so without paying a price in terms of the credibility of its future word and of the respect of other nations—both of which are of some, if varying, importance to all nations. The fact that the Soviets had broken the previous moratorium was held against them and against the nuclear testban treaty in some quarters; this was outweighed only by recognition that, with their previous bad reputation, the Soviets would find their word beyond any belief should they violate such a written treaty and would therefore probably be further deterred from doing so by this consideration.

As a projection into the future, there are four important aspects to the substance of an international agreement. First, it is a prediction of future worlds and events. It may sometimes be desirable to make the provisions for the future in an agreement vague or even misleading. But unless such a condition is intentional, it may jeopardize the longevity of the agreement. It seems likely that one reason for the short life expectancy of most arms control proposals is their inadequate attention to this aspect. For instance, a disarmament treaty which fails to describe concretely the disarming and disarmed world is rightly viewed with suspicion in most cautious quarters.

Second, just as an international agreement is a prediction of the good deeds of the signatories, so is it ideally a projection of the way in which these good deeds will bring about the predicted future. In other words, it is a statement of means as well as of ends. The importance of this aspect to the viability of an agreement should be clear. It is not necessarily ideal to specify all the means or the only admissible means to the end. But such specification should be omitted only consciously and deliberately. Examples of failure to state means are not hard to find: One was the Kellogg-Briand Pact. Enumeration of means is not necessarily good and sufficient, for such documents as the United Nations Charter incorporate considerable specification of means but are rendered largely ineffective by the unrealistic means they specify. Similarly, a general and comprehensive disarmament agreement that specifies that order would be kept by an international police force in tomorrow's world would be dangerously visionary in its projection of means.

Third, an international agreement is a complex of incentives. Traditionally, descriptions of agreements emphasize the penalties for certain actions; only rarely do such descriptions emphasize the *rewards* of agreement. In many agreements, the sanctions to be applied for noncompliance are more prominent than the rewards for compliance. And it is possible that past agreements have not given rewards their deserved attention. For example, there is the obvious reward of the success of the agreement if both sides comply. But if only one side complies, it has little to gain and much to lose in many agreements, particularly in most proposed arms control treaties. It should be possible, especially in complex and comprehensive agreements like disarmament treaties, to build in rewards for compliance, especially for unilateral compliance, just as it is often suggested that there be built in punishments for noncompliance. This possibility will be further developed when controls are considered in Chapter 6.

A final aspect of the international agreement as a projection is its role as a prospect—the prospect of further agreement if the original agreement is successful. It is probably true that the success of one agreement will encourage contemplation and perhaps even negotiation of further agreements, particularly if they are similar. Thus, the continued successful operation of the limited nuclear testban treaty encouraged advocacy of extension to underground tests and even elaboration to a nonproliferation agreement. But it is doubtful that success alone, apart from enabling political conditions and national interests, would bring about further agreements. The important point may be more strongly expressed in the negative, for the most significant impact of one agreement upon the prospects for another is likely to be the preclusive effect of a broken first agreement upon further agreement.

This consideration can become another compliance incentive to participating nations, not because they have further agreements that they are anxious to achieve, but because they cannot be certain in a revolutionary and nuclear age that they can afford to seriously lessen the possibility of reaching further agreements at some later point when perhaps unforeseen difficulties or challenges arise. For this reason, if none other, the prospect of further agreement is an important aspect of any significant international agreement.

The differences in importance of these various aspects of what has been called the "nonspecific substance" of any international agreement are generally obvious. That an agreement is a complex of incentives is more important in most cases than that it is a statement of the good word and good faith of the signatories, for example. But neither analysts nor proposers have given adequate conceptual attention to the nonspecific substance that will characterize any international agreement whether they are fully aware of it or not. It should become clearer in the analysis of maintenance of arms control in Chapter 7 that opportunities for more promising exploitation of the fact of international agreement can be lost because this analytical work has not been done and because its implications have not been developed and applied with greater depth and thoughtfulness.

The Elements of an International Agreement

More specific than these aspects of the substance of any international agreement are the elements of an agreement. These elements will include procedures by which the agreement is to be ratified and implemented, as well as substantive provisions such as specified arms controls. The preceding chapter considered arms controls achieved through tacit negotiation. This chapter will focus upon agreements resulting in treaties or other formal verbal statements, because the elements which will characterize any agreements are more easily analyzed in cases where they are explicit and extensive. A brief enumeration of these elements will emphasize the range to be covered or considered in creating a promising international agreement.

The basic procedures of treaty making are clear. After credentials are exchanged the treaty is drafted. Although the negotiators sign the completed draft treaty, ratification waits on the action of the highest executive sovereign of each signatory; such ratification is frequently "preceded" by "advice and consent" or other permissive action by a national legislature. When the instruments of ratification have been exchanged by the signatories, the treaty is in force, and its actual execution or implementation is then brought about. There may be opportunities to exploit or alter these procedures to contribute promise to the creation and achievement of an international agreement on a complex subject like arms control. Among the possibilities to be considered are staging of provisions, or of ratification, and even of accession, as well as controlled permission of reservations.

Considerable attention is often given to the exploitation of the opportunities for including provisions and visions in an agreement, but slight attention is given to comparable opportunities for exclusion. Although the invocation of the Deity and the preliminary pledge of perpetual peace, which characterized treaties made through the eighteenth century, have disappeared, three other basic elements continue to characterize most treaties: the simple preamble setting forth the general purposes of the agreement and giving the names of the signatories; the articles which form the body of the agreement; and a statement of the conditions of ratification.

The explicit inclusions in a treaty will be its provisions. There is, however, one type of treaty that lacks such specific provisions: the *pactum de contrahendo*. This is an agreement by a state to conclude a later and final agreement. It is no longer often used, although it was used for Articles 93, 284, and 354 of the Versailles Treaty. There persists dispute as to whether the obligation incurred by signatories of such a *pactum* is simply to undertake negotiations or is to reach agreement. It is of interest in arms control negotiations because of the possible role of intentional ambiguity, the tactic of postponing difficult questions, and the problems of specification, which will be examined in Chapter 6.[2]

An early provision of a typical treaty is a statement of the objectives of the agreement. Equally preliminary is a description of the organization of the agreement, that is, what nations participate, under what auspices, and in what roles (as sovereign independent states, as members of an alliance, as friendly nations, or otherwise). Another element is the provision for administration of the agreement. The most widely appreciated element is the statement of promised action or of promised inaction or of both. In addition, there may or may not be a

[2]On the *pactum de contrahendo* see Arnold Duncan (Lord) McNair, *The Law of Treaties* (New York: Oxford University Press, 1961), pp. 27–29. This book is also a useful source for and discussion of many other aspects of treaty law.

record of incentives (usually punishments but occasionally rewards). Another optional element is a statement of the procedures for termination, extension, amendment, or other alteration of previous provisions. Finally come the ratification provisions.[3]

No agreement must have all these provisions, but any important international agreement concerning a complex issue like arms control will probably have most of them. And the absence of any one of these fundamental provisions can be viewed as an act of exclusion, which in itself would be significant. Not only the inclusions, but also the exclusions in an international agreement deserve mention. Explicit exclusions are generally quite obvious, taking the form of stated exceptions, waivers, and other provisions. They may also, however, take the form of exclusions of certain of the basic provisions just enumerated, such as those for incentives or amendment.

Implicit exclusions are difficult to discover and more misleading to analyze. The common-sense assumption is dangerous: That which is not included is thereby excluded. Because an international agreement covering an important political issue will necessarily be highly complex, it will be difficult to include adequate and comprehensive statement of those aspects on which the signatories are wholly in accord. And because any international agreement must cope with an uncertain future as well as a complex present, it will be difficult to incorporate provisions that will of themselves provide clear and acceptable terms for future behavior. Again, beyond these problems there is the challenge of coping with those areas of the international situation that are consequential to a comprehensive and sound agreement but upon which agreement has not, and perhaps at the time cannot, be reached. These problems will be examined in Chapter 7.

Once again, it appears difficult to speak conclusively about the nature and scope of the elements of an international agreement. Major international political problems become increasingly complex and consequential, and agreements to cope with them must become correspondingly comprehensive and effective. And while an agreement's elements always provide some capacity for development of the more technical, technological, and engineering aspects, it seems unlikely that this capacity will be sufficient to meet increasingly greater and complex demands. Consequently, analysts and proposers will likely be forced to turn to the more procedural and substantive aspects, if international agreement, especially in the challenging area of arms control, is to be a better prospect and a greater promise.

[3]Each of these elements will be examined as possible inclusions in an arms control agreement in Chapters 6 and 7.

The Nature of the International Agreement

The provisions and their acceptance and implementation will arise out of the agreement process, or treaty-making process. The selection of measures, the determination of their elements, and their construction into the provisions of the international agreement are all determined in the course of negotiation and expressed thereafter by drafting (if the agreement is written), by declaration, or by activity (if the agreement is to be tacitly enacted).

Ideally, the selection of measures will be determined by cumulated national objectives. In fact, selection is likely to be highly influenced by acceptability, possibility, and salience of measures common to men's minds. Once the subject matter of agreement is selected, determination of the elements to be included will probably be more deliberate and objective-oriented. The painstaking negotiation over the verification provisions of the testban treaty is probably typical. The elements combine to institutionalize the measures. The general elements characterizing any international agreement include objectives, organization, administration, incentives, ratification, elaboration, specification, alteration, extension, and termination. These and other elements and how they relate to arms control agreements will be examined in detail in Chapters 6 and 7.

In an international agreement, the subject matter and the elements of institutionalization must be assembled, by drafting or action, to form the actual provisions of the agreement to be accepted. Stated elliptically, the basic provisions of an agreement are a description of a desired world and a collection of promises by each participant to act so as to create that world if the provisions function as expected and thereby encourage other nations to do so as well. In this context, Hedley Bull's contention that "the purpose of multilateral disarmament negotiations is jointly to remove the anxieties that are an obstacle to unilateral disarmament"[4] is insightful. The challenge is to construct arms control agreements that will create conditions in which nations will want to disarm. Such agreements can be conceived. They must be well constructed, and they must either possess the necessary "teeth" or be embraced with impressive general compliance. But to be either, they must first be found acceptable to those nations that are potential participants to the international agreement.

It is sometimes suggested that provisions can be substituted for by, or at least temporarily replaced by, "trust." It is difficult enough to

[4]Hedley Bull, *Control of the Arms Race* (London: Weidenfield and Nicolson, 1961), p. 89.

determine just what is the nature of trust. But discovering wherein such trust might reside in international intercourse is even more difficult. Trust may be viewed as a condition of investment in the object coupled with a feeling of confidence in that object. The contention that one must have trust in one's adversary is misleading. One can "trust" his adversary to act in his own interests, although even that can be risky—nations sometimes do not perceive clearly their own interests and they are not always the best judges of the perceived interests of other nations. And one can "trust" one's own military establishment to act and be able to act in accordance with one's directives in terms of its capabilities. But fundamentally, in the case of agreed arms control, one trusts the agreement itself. In many significant aspects, the agreement must replace the military establishment, which is being limited in serving to defend the country. (This will be elaborated upon in Chapter 9.) This is why the construction of an arms control agreement is such a serious and often dangerous undertaking. And it helps to explain why nations are reluctant to accept arms control proposals: They are asked to commit themselves and their successors to act differently than they otherwise would, simply because there exists an agreement with other nations which provides that they too will act differently in prescribed ways. And even more burdensome and ominous, the nations are generally asked to commit themselves to a series of progressive activities often extending far into the future.

But must this long-term bulk commitment necessarily characterize acceptance of an arms control agreement? It has become traditional for draft treaties on "general and complete disarmament" to contain three stages. Dispute in negotiation concerns the nature of each stage, rather than the ways in which the concept and technique of staging could best be applied in the creating of arms control agreements. Of course, staging is not always useful. The limited nuclear testban would not have benefited appreciably from substantive staging, although had it also banned underground tests such a provision might usefully have been made a second stage in the agreement. Major economic, political, and military agreements are more likely candidates for staging. The experience of the European Economic Community is instructive, for staging of degree in tariff equalization, as well as staging of kind in types of goods—and also, if general language in the treaty and the expressed desires of some parties are to be believed, in the movement from economic to political unification—has permitted relatively steady progress in the negotiation and implementation of integration to which nations could not have acceded unconditionally at the outset.

The obvious place for employment of the staging principle is in design or drafting of the substantive provisions for arms control. Staging focuses attention upon the desirability of designing stages to achieve acceptable balance among participants. It also emphasizes the importance of stage-by-stage compliance by participants, and it raises the possibility of national use of ratification to encourage or discourage comparable behavior by other nations. A major difficulty in the design of arms control proposals has been developing stages at each of which all nations can continue to have confidence in the agreement because their security forces are balanced with those of possible adversaries and allies. This does not mean that they are necessarily equivalent, but rather that levels are acceptable to each participant. Such problems of balance would be lessened if each stage were smaller, in other words, if there were not three but thirteen or thirty stages provided in the major agreement. In that case, each stage could be reached more rapidly with less potential imbalancing change, both required and unexpected, and hence less intrinsic danger for the participants. It is probably true that many of the problems in negotiating three stages would be multiplied in negotiating thirteen or thirty, for difficulties of measurement and commensuration as well as transition could reside in each stage. But because the scope and consequences of each stage would be considerably less, national reluctance might also be less.

If a multitude of stages were provided, they might all be negotiated and signed at the same time, but then ratified individually (as if they were separate treaties) on any one of a number of principles to be considered below. Or they might be negotiated over the course of progressive arms control, so as to cope better with unforeseen problems and changing national desires and commitments.

The nature of such stages would be determined basically by the interplay of national security considerations. Thus, nuclear weapons would be retained as long as their deterrent effect would be desirable, as has finally been recognized and granted by the Soviet Union in the Geneva negotiations. Another important determinant might be remembrance that nations are more apt to accept an agreement if there is less to accept at first; that is, if there is an implicit "way out" through failing to proceed further with negotiation and ratification rather than only through failing to comply with previous commitments. In addition, nations would probably be more apt to accept an agreement if its road ahead were somewhat visible. Thus, while it would be possible to negotiate stages step-by-step after an initial agreement that does little more than to provide for such continual negotiation and perhaps to specify the approximate number of stages envisaged, this would probably be less desired.

Nonetheless, this progressive, piecemeal approach would recognize and anticipate another important consideration: the difficulty of achieving specificity in stages projected far into the future without straight-jacketing participating nations if bans are open-ended or without straight-jacketing the agreement itself and its information and control organs if permissions are open-ended. These problems of specificity and ambiguity (which will be examined in more detail in Chapter 7) are primarily problems of drafting and imply that perhaps drafting itself should be staged in accord with such features as degree of compliance, changes in the international system, and technological and military developments. It would be foolhardy to pretend that all such features could be adequately coped with by staged drafting, just as it would be foolhardy to presume that they could be satisfactorily anticipated in a major agreement drafted in one prolonged sitting before any implementation. More likely to be successful would be drafting that became less specific as time was projected, but which nonetheless specified limits and guidelines, as well as machinery and principles for further future negotiation.

If little attention has been given to substantive stages, far less has been devoted to the staging of ratification and accession. Signature, ratification, and compliance are three distinct early stages in the life cycle of an international agreement. If an agreement were a staged progression, each stage might be negotiated in a separate treaty, but all stage treaties might be negotiated and signed at the same time. Nations could then ratify each stage treaty in accordance with one of various principles or requirements. They could be required to ratify all stages at once, either at the outset of the control process or upon joining the agreement. This is comparable to the standard procedure. Or ratification could take place in stages: Upon completion of each stage, the next might be ratified and then implemented.

A more intriguing provision would be that ratification was to take place at the will of participants, perhaps within specified maximal time limits. This would allow nations to use ratification as a way of expressing good will or confidence in the agreement and thereby, perhaps, encourage other recalcitrant nations to ratify also through the use of ratification as an "initiative" to overcome mutual inertia. The price that an overly trusting and ratifying nation might pay were such initiatives to fail might be substantial, but it seems unlikely that nations would take grave risks. Moreover, risks could be minimized by multiplication of stages, so that each step would be small. If one or another such staged ratification plan or any of the multitude of variants conceivable were in effect, some of the immense problems of providing for complete future equity at the time of first drafting might be averted or lessened. And national attention might be shifted somewhat from concern with meticulous equality to concern with the prolonged effective functioning of the arms control measure.

With such staging, nations might desire to attach reservations to their ratification. Some agreements might usefully allow compliance conditional, not simply upon the adherence and compliance of others (which will often qualify a nation's actions), but also upon other actions by other nations or even upon the development of the nation's own posture. And reservations might be accepted by other parties to the agreement, as frequently has been the case in previous international security treaties, such as the Versailles Treaty and the Kellogg-Briand Pact. Allowance of reservations and recognition of conditions can easily vitiate an agreement, particularly if it deals with national security affairs on which nations are particularly reluctant to agree to binding limitations. On the other hand, open recognition of the national interests in such reservation and conditional commitment again focuses attention on the importance of designing an arms control agreement to serve the individual as well as the collective interests in security.

If the view of each participant, it may be that the general good of the agreement can overbalance particular distasteful or undesirable features. If that is so and if the particular features contribute to the developing international provisions for mutual security, these features are probably worth encouraging by not allowing reservation. But if achievement of an arms control agreement that is acceptable to all participants must rest upon conditions and reservations, provisions may be desirable—particularly if they are temporally limited (as were some provisions of the European Economic Community regulations) or if they seem subject to change and elimination as nations redesign their security establishments in accord with the arms control agreement.

A further provision that would contribute to the acceptability and longevity of an arms control agreement would allow for deratification of a stage; or perhaps there could even be a provision in the basic agreement for withdrawal by a nation that was no longer prepared to accept it. Article 4 of the testban treaty contains a clause permitting such withdrawal:

This Treaty shall be of unlimited duration. Each Party shall in exercising its national sovereignty have the right to withdraw from the Treaty if it decides that extraordinary events, related to the subject matter of this Treaty, have jeopardized the supreme interests of its country. It shall give notice of such withdrawal to all other Parties to the Treaty three months in advance.

Such permission of preannounced withdrawal might be allowed to a nation that had ratified the whole of a treaty that was then not complied with in part by another or to a nation that had ratified a stage which was not subsequently accepted by another. The sense of such permission would be to allow a nation the possibility of responding to such dereliction by another without necessarily rejecting or withdrawing from the entire agreement.

Withdrawal or partial rejection need not be made dependent upon previous failings by another nation. Reconsideration of individual national security and objectives (including internal police needs) or changes in the technological bases of a nation's defense forces might provide occasions for unilateral deratification of a stage of provision of the general agreement. Whether such deratification would be allowed without approval by the administrative organ or the adjudicative organ, although, perhaps, with specified notice to other adherents, would be provided in the basic agreement. Such allowance, both to encourage reluctant nations to accept the agreement and to discourage unhappy nations from destroying the entire agreement should it break down in part, merits careful consideration.

A final aspect of the attainment of arms control is accession or adhesion to the treaty.[5] The testban treaty was left open to subsequent accession by any nations conforming to its ratification specifications. Such a procedure is not uncommon with a generalized agreement. But accession can be made easier if provisions for graduated accession (such as those envisaged when Great Britain was negotiating to join the European Economic Community) are incorporated into the agreement, so that late-awakening nations may join avant-garde nations in submitting their military establishments to limitation in the service of national and multinational security. In addition, the agreement might be staged so that it first applies only to the superpowers, who perhaps undertook joint limitation at levels where other nations were not involved. It could later be extended to the would-be great powers. And then, when arms

⁵The problem of accession to disarmament agreements is discussed very generally in Fred C. Ikle, *Alternative Approaches to the International Organization of Disarmament* (Santa Monica, Calif.: RAND Corporation, 1961), appendix C, pp. 41–44.

levels and military characteristics of those nations reach a level of concern to the larger powers, the lesser powers might be invited (or perhaps more strongly encouraged) to join, complying with provisions either negotiated earlier or deferred until they became significant. Such an "open-sided" agreement, staged temporally and substantively by "categories" of states, would provide eventually for weakling nations as well as superpowers, thereby developing a more general nature as time and the control of military establishments progressed. The likelihood that such a generalized and comprehensive arms control agreement could be reached in the near future is, of course, slight at best. But provision for its possibility and thought about its possible nature are not uncalled for in view of the increasing importance of more universal arms control agreements.

Many if not most of the aspects of attaining arms control discussed here—particularly those arising out of ratification, reservation, and accession—may appear far-projected and, to some perhaps, far-fetched. Examination of the determinants of national interest in arms control suggests that attaining any agreements at all would be difficult; that attaining written agreements (in which many of these aspects would be more relevant and to which many of these propositions might be more adaptable) might prove harder still; and that attaining generalized and comprehensive agreements (in which many of these aspects could prove crucial to the success of the agreement) might prove totally impossible. Such processes as ratification and accession are essential elements in many international agreements, in fact if not always in form, and thus merit careful consideration in an examination of arms control. However, they can only permit passage to implementation of an agreement. And it is problems of implementation and maintenance which are most likely to prohibit the successful functioning—or even attainment—of an international arms control agreement.

CHAPTER 6

The Implementation
of Arms Control

Many of the problems that will arise in approaching and attaining an important international arms control agreement are intensified by anticipation of difficulties in implementing and maintaining the agreement in the face of change both in nations and in their environs. An arms control agreement will be subject to two different challenges: internal strain and external stress. The parties themselves may seek to bend the agreement to their own interests. Indeed, this could be characterized as a natural tendency in nations. Once agreement is achieved—that is, once the provisions of the agreement have been constructed and ratification has been obtained—implementation of an arms control agreement will almost certainly raise problems of administration, adjudication, information, control, and extension or termination. These problems will be consequences of internal strain on the agreement and will call for employment of implementation provisions which are the subject of this chapter. Furthermore, given such change in nations and environments, there will arise the necessity for application and probably innovation of provisions for maintenance of the agreement in the face of external stress—the subject of analysis in Chapter 7.

The organs and procedures for implementation, designed to anticipate the necessities and cope with the problems mentioned above, will generally be described in the agreement itself, but some agreements lack such provisions. Thus, the nuclear testban treaty provides only for termination. However, in this treaty, verification and control provisions are implied: Verification is to be undertaken unilaterally by adversaries with whatever means are available and mutually accepted; control is by the sanction of possible responsive noncompliance. Similarly, when an agreement is of such a limited character that the participants can be satisfied by implicit and hence limited provisions for verification and control, ease of attainment and acceptability will probably suggest the use of implicit provisions. But even in cases where provisions are explicit and multiple, implementation need not necessarily be a grave problem if the machinery and procedures are well created and well established and if the cumulated national determinants which have been analyzed earlier exist and persist. There are five major areas with which implementation provisions may deal: administration, adjudication, information, control, and extension and termination.

Administration

The specific manifestations of the general problems of administration (such as authority, responsibilities, powers, funds, organization, and decision rules and procedures) cannot be considered apart from the substance of the arms control agreement and the organs created to implement information and control provisions; specific provisions for administration are directly related to requirements contained in other provisions, especially those for adjudication or interpretation, inspection and verification, and control. But, in general, the administrative aspect of an arms control agreement will include such important functions as finance, staffing, direction, communication, and planning.

Finance, an often neglected aspect of arms control, will include cost allocation, cost collection, and budgeting. Financial aspects have probably been neglected because thus far arms control arrangements have involved either no transnational financing (the limited testban) or little national financing (the hotline), and because the belief is still widespread that arms control would be less costly than unrestricted arming activity—a view that is not necessarily correct.[1]

Agreement upon cost-sharing provisions could prove difficult, for this would require generalized determination of ability to pay and perhaps of benefits received based upon such yardsticks as national income or defense spending, which are at best unclear and incommensurable and which will raise again the questions of "troika" and other models of international resources and responsibilities.[2] In this event,

[1]See Thomas C. Schelling and Morton H. Halperin, *Strategy and Arms Control* (New York: Twentieth Century, 1961), chap. 11; and Thomas C. Schelling, "Arms Control Will Not Cut Defense Costs," *Harvard Business Review,* March (1961).

[2]See Thomas C. Schelling, "International Cost-Sharing Arrangements," *Essays in International Finance,* 24 (Princeton, N. J.: International Finance Section, Department of Economics and Sociology of Princeton University, 1955); Oskar Morgenstern, "Military Alliance and Mutual Security," in David M. Abshire and

cost apportionment—a sort of functional allocation comparable to the financing of the hotline, in which each party undertakes certain costs regardless of their eventual magnitude—might be attempted. Such an approach might avert or lessen the ominous difficulties inherent in the international budgetary approach which international organizations, like the United Nations, have had to employ and which entail determinations of shares as well as allocation of accumulated resources to specific projects. Efforts might be made to create relatively independent sources of revenue for the international administration organ, such as property rights to sacrificed and debilitated weapons that can be marketed as scrap or rental revenue rights to abandoned military bases. In any event, no single source of revenue or approach to revenue is likely to prove adequate and dependable enough to finance the potentially gigantic costs of information and control activities or to finance international research on improved inspection, verification, and control as would probably be required by substantial disarmament. Fortunately, the financial aspects of many lesser measures are not as important or sizable.

A second aspect of importance, varying with the scope of the measure, is staffing of the administrative, information, control, and adjudicatory organs. The principles of staffing would probably be established by the parties to the agreement. Most postwar Western proposals have referred to impartial, neutral, or international servants; Soviet proposals, which reflect disbelief that there can be impartial internationals, have mentioned the use of nationals or combinations of nationals and adversaries. Once such principles of organization and personnel selection have been established and the administrative organ has been staffed, there will be further staffing of the other organs created by the agreement, as well as continual restaffing.[3]

A third and fundamental administrative function will be direction—policy implementation through supervision and coordination of the activities of other organs, particularly the verification and control organs, depending upon the authority, responsibilities, and powers of each organ.

Richard V. Allen (eds.), *National Security: Political, Military, and Economic Strategies in the Decade Ahead* (New York: Praeger, 1963), pp. 671–686; and John Pincus, *Economic Aid and International Cost Sharing* (R-431-15A. Santa Monica, Calif.: RAND Corporation, 1965), chaps. 3 and 4.

[3]See Fred C. Ikle, *Alternative Approaches to the International Organization of Disarmament* (Santa Monica, Calif.: RAND Corporation, 1961), and Lincoln P. Bloomfield, *The Politics of Arms Control: Troika, Veto, and International Institutions* (Washington, D.C.: Institute for Defense Analyses, 1961).

A fourth function will be communication of requirements, decisions, progress, and regress to participants and to the other organs.

And the fifth fundamental administrative task will be planning. While most planning will concern the other four functions and their manifestation in adjudication, information, and control, some planning will be concerned with maintenance activities: accession, elaboration and specification, and alteration. (These maintenance activities will be considered in detail in Chapter 7.) The extent and importance of such planning will depend upon the discretionary power that the administrative organ is provided with or allowed to exert and will probably be subject to considerable restraint by participant nations.

In the execution of each of these functions, the problem of rules and procedures for decision making will arise and thus must have been provided for. Procedures for voting (whether the method is individual or collective; whether the mechanism is unanimity, majority, plurality, or unit-veto voting; and whether voting is in some way weighted) and for determination of the agenda could play decisive roles in determining the outcome of disputes and conflicts of interest in the administrative organ and in other authoritative organs. Although formal provisions often prove to be circumventable, such circumvention is at best costly and at worst pernicious in its threat to undermine the bases of the agreement.[4]

These administrative functions will arise from an agreement requiring the establishment of some sort of "international disarmament organization," as most recent proposals by Russia and the United States have termed it. The composition of this organization is usually conceived of as similar to the United Nations: Director General with Secretariat, Permanent Commission to select composition similar to the Security Council, and General Assembly of all participants.[5] Its relation to the United Nations is undetermined, although some contend

[4]Several works on the theory of voting and decision were cited in Chapter 5. Relevant here also are two studies by Cromwell A. Riches, *The Unanimity Rule and the League of Nations* (Baltimore: Johns Hopkins Press, 1933), and *Majority Rule in International Organizations: A Study of the Trend from Unanimity to Majority Decision* (Baltimore: Johns Hopkins Press, 1940). Riches found a great number of ingenious devices by which the League organs, especially the Assembly, had escaped the rigors of the restrictive unanimity rule.

[5]Such a conception, first put forward in the French working paper of September 2, 1955, has since been adopted in general form by both Russia and the United States. See the various proposals reprinted in the USACDA's *Documents on Disarmament* series (Washington, D.C.: Government Printing Office, 1960 to date).

that the United Nations should be made into such an organ and thereby somehow strengthened.

The very size and complexity of the administrative organ itself would depend upon the nature of the arms control to be undertaken and the acceptability at that time of international machinery to participants. If the agreement were of quite limited scope, its administrative machinery could be limited more easily. And if the agreement involved only a small number of powers or did not become general until a late stage in its progress, its administrative organ might consist entirely in a Security Council-like organ with a Director General or Chairman and a small staff. Thus, the administrative functions and organs discussed here might be minimized or latent, if needed at all, in some arms control arrangements.

Adjudication

Another aspect of implementation that could prove important to the development and persistence of a substantial arms control agreement is adjudication. In cases of uncertainty or dispute, there will be need and opportunity for interpretation of the agreement itself. Such examination would probably be in terms of the intention of the parties, as expressed in the words used by them in the light of the surrounding circumstances;[6] and it might be in the context of applicable international legal provisions, such as the principle of *rebus sic stantibus*.

Disputes about the interpretation of an agreement will almost certainly be manifest in action and inaction by the participants. A nation, accused by another nation or by an arms control organ of being noncompliant, would probably offer its own interpretation of the requirements and promises to be found in the treaty, just as nations continue to explain and justify behavior in terms of their conceptions of international law. But although some disputes might originate in "honest" differences of interpretation, others might originate in efforts to circumvent requirements and break promises and yet might be manifest in alleged variant interpretations. Control provisions, to be considered later in this chapter, would be very important in most cases of noncompliance. Such controls, if they were *ex post* enforcement rather than *ex ante* regulation, would probably wait on judicial deter-

[6]This formulation of the nature of treaty interpretation is put forth and defended by Arnold Duncan (Lord) McNair in his *The Law of Treaties,* chap. 20.

mination of default and might wait forever on a nation no longer interested in preserving the agreement. But there might well arise cases in which nations desirous of cheating, once caught, would be prepared to accept adjudicated consequences and let the agreement's provisions resume sway because, on balance, they preferred the agreement's continuation to its termination.

There are, then, three basic types of ruling which might be required in the implementation of an arms control agreement. The first is that of the *meaning* of the agreement—its requirements and promises—which corresponds to the product of the traditional interpretive function of courts in treaty law. The second is that of *action*—determination of what has and has not been done, the major role in which would be undertaken by the information organ. And the third is that of the *correspondence* of meaning and action—the question of compliance.

If the adjudicatory organ is to undertake interpretation of the agreement and assessment of compliance, the kinds of cases it will encounter would include: disputes between two or more states over interpretation; disputes between an agreement organ and a state about the state's performance; disputes between one state and another (joined as defendant, perhaps by the agreement organ) about that other's performance where the organ did not hold noncompliance; requests by the agreement organ to undertake further verification steps or enforcement activities against a state found noncompliant; appeals by a state against determinations by the organ on such grounds as lack of competence, procedural violations, or abuse of power; and appeals by private persons against decisions by the agreement organ's enforcement of the threat against them and perhaps unjustifiably injuring them.[7]

Such adjudication is distinguishable, in theory if perhaps not always in fact, from decision in cases of nonjusticiable, discretionary resolution of conflict where there is neither text nor precedential activity to interpret. Nonetheless, even where the action is quite clearly adjudication, human judgment and discretion must play a role. Because such adjudication tends to focus upon procedural and legalistic aspects in interpreting the provisions of an agreement, it can encourage "fractionation" of conflict—breaking up big issues into little ones. As Roger

[7]Most of these cases and considerable specific material on the possible nature and composition of adjudicatory agencies are contained in Louis Sohn's "Adjudication and Enforcement in Arms Control" in Donald Brennan (ed.), *Arms Control, Disarmament, and National Security* (New York: Braziller, 1961), pp. 365–375.

Fisher has suggested, "Viewed from this perspective, adjudication appears not as a process for settling big conflicts, but rather as one that is valuable because it tends to fragment conflict situations by cutting off and serving up for decision one small issue at a time."[8] But such procedural and legalistic resolutions are possible in large part because they abstract from most political bases of the dispute. And if those political bases are broad enough, adjudicatory settlement might do more harm than good.

To avert collapse, adjudication might be undertaken before the agreement breaks down. But agreement might also be undertaken after one side has failed to comply with provisions in order to gain a unilateral advantage or after one side has complied in a way or to an extent that has entailed unilateral sacrifice. In such cases, adjudication could serve to determine negative or positive sanctions that might permit continuation of the agreement despite temporary breakdown. The great challenge is to make this decision upon sanctions, following breakdown or lapse, so automatic that it is found preferable to the traditional "self-help" response.

The effectiveness of adjudication will depend in part upon the nature of the organ undertaking it. Settlement of disputes by adjudication differs from settlement by war or by bargaining in that it involves a "settler." The prominent existing adjudicatory settler in international affairs is the International Court of Justice. Some postwar disarmament proposals by Western nations have suggested that the International Court be relied upon, or at least appealed to, for advisory opinions in cases of justiciable disputes during the disarmament process. It might also be found desirable to use national courts, as is done in some international disputes, in cases where verification or control provisions entail national action in compliance with treaty-made regulations.[9]

On the other hand, it might be desirable to ignore the highly legalistic precedents and records of failure constructed over many years in international legal tribunals and to ignore, perhaps, the provisions of international law themselves by creating an independent ongoing body

[8]Roger Fisher, "Fractionating Conflict," in Roger Fisher (ed.), *International Conflict and Behavioral Science: The Craigville Papers* (New York: Basic Books, 1964), p. 92.

[9]See Roger Fisher, "Internal Enforcement of International Rules" in Seymour Melman (ed.), *Disarmament: Its Politics and Economics* (Boston: American Academy of Arts and Sciences, 1962), pp. 99–120; and Louis Henkin, *Arms Control and Inspection in American Law* (New York: Columbia University Press, 1958).

or system of courts intended to settle treaty disputes judicially in terms of the treaty alone or by constituting a special arbitral body by agreement among the parties whenever a dispute arises. But regardless of the approach and organ, adjudication, which may prove essential in implementing a treaty drafted by mortal and elliptical men, is unlikely to be able to cope adequately with all problems of interpretation and application of the treaty provisions. Recognized needs for specification and alteration will encourage eventual reliance upon an extralegal interpretive and expansive body for maintenance of the agreement, as will be discussed in Chapter 7.

Information

Another fundamental aspect of an arms control measure will be its provisions for information. This aspect is often referred to as "inspection," but this term, even when employed in a general sense, is somewhat misleading and too narrow for the phenomena that it is intended to describe.

Most information gathering takes place without a grant of access and without the acquiescence or cooperation of the country being studied. Such unilateral employment of open sources within the country, of observant forces outside it, and of covert operations everywhere could be termed "monitoring." The information provisions of the nuclear testban treaty concern monitoring alone. However, most provisions for information in proposed disarmament treaties are grounded in grants of access, whether to international forces or to adversary forces. Such grants of access may authorize outsiders to enter an area to confirm that the government has done what it claims to have done or such grants may authorize outside forces to examine not only what has been done, but also what may have been left undone or done covertly. The former case is likely to be a "one-shot" examination of a certain activity or disposition. This is what the Soviet Union means when it refers to "inspection of disarmament" (in effect, watching the weapons be destroyed), but is more properly termed "verification." In the latter case, examination of things done and undone, within the limits of relevance, will be a continual operation. This is what the Western nations mean when they refer to "inspection of disarmament" and what the Russians refer to, in a sense quite properly, as "inspection of armament." It is appropriately termed "inspection." The term "information" is used here to include monitoring, verification, and inspection—the totality of means by which one nation might determine whether another is complying with its obligations under the arms control agreement.[10]

This information aspect would serve several important functions in the implementation and maintenance of an arms control agreement. The actions undertaken in the name of information—mostly verification and inspection for monitoring is constantly carried out by all nations—will detect violation of the agreement or they will fail to detect violation, in which case the implication (which may be quite false) will be that there has been no violation. Thus, these actions bring about knowledge—or, more accurately, belief—about violation and compliance especially, but also probably about other aspects of the military establishments of other nations. This bonus information, primarily a result of monitoring and inspection, might be viewed as a side benefit of the basic information process, whether it is specifically provided for or not. Such side benefits are desired mostly because the placement of controls upon one aspect of the military establishment will probably shift adversary attention as well as national activity to other military aspects, and this will raise further concern about national security and the international military balance. Thus, in effect, such bonus information, whether the product of inspection, of monitoring, or of espionage, may provide what a nation will need to know, beyond information about compliance with and violation of specific provisions, in order to remain satisfied with the agreement.

But verification and inspection, if adequate and effective, can serve other functions. First, their existence reassures participants in an agreement that no evasion is presently taking place and that any cheating that might have occurred will be detected. In addition, it is often said that these provisions deter evasion, but this reasoning disguises the actual effect, which is to encourage compliance.

The encouragement to comply is manifest in the implication, confirmed by the information process, that the adversary is complying. Because of this, it will be safer for a nation to comply than it would

[10]These distinctions are well made by Charles Burton Marshall in his article "Hide and Seek: Dour Thoughts on Inspection," *The New Republic,* Nov. 24 (1962), pp. 14–17. Reproduced in a pamphlet, *Cuba: Thoughts Prompted by the Crisis* (Washington Center of Foreign Policy Research, Washington, D.C., 1962), written after the Cuban missile crisis and based upon work done at the Woods Hole Summer Study of Verification and Response administered by the Institute for Defense Analyses. Following the usage in that study, Marshall uses the word "verification" as the general term for monitoring, inspection, and what he calls "authentication." Usage in general supports the specific use of "verification," for one cannot verify a fact; he can only verify a statement.

otherwise be; and what might be justified as "defensive noncompliance" (protection against the possibility of the adversary's noncompliance) is less necessary, if even perhaps more tempting because of the unilateral advantage it might produce.

The encouragement to comply is also manifest in the intimation that noncompliance would be detected, raising the possibility of a response that might terminate the benefits of the agreement and even bring about application of negative sanctions. These considerations will weigh differently with different nations, depending upon their assessment of the undesirability of such responses and the likelihood of each.

In addition to encouraging compliance, information provisions would also encourage participants to demonstrate their compliance in order to avoid the possible consequences of mistaken beliefs that a nation has broken the agreement. One possible and dangerous consequence of such misconceptions would be undesired "responses to violation." But even if such a misconception did not come to such action, it would bring about exacerbated tensions, something which the arms control agreement would be in part intended to avert. In addition, misconceptions of noncompliance would waste time and effort and obstruct the normal functioning of the information, administration, and perhaps even control organs of the agreement until the misunderstandings were straightened out.

The incentive to demonstrate compliance will be an important feature of most arms control measures and has led Schelling and Halperin to suggest the possibility of substantial arms control agreement wholly lacking in formal information provisions and grounded in the happy conjunction of the "show-me" attitude of each participant and the reciprocal desire to show as long as the agreement is mutually desired.[11] Should nations not wish to rely entirely upon this reciprocal interest in sufficient demonstration of compliance, they would at least be wise to design information provisions of arms control agreements to facilitate such voluntary evidence.

The specific provisions of the information aspects of an agreement will also contribute to the definition of possible responses to violations, particularly because they will be important determinants of how much a nation will learn about violation and compliance, how quickly, and how easily. The more knowledge a nation is able to obtain, both about the general pattern of compliance in other cases and about the specific

[11]See Thomas C. Schelling and Morton H. Halperin, *Strategy and Arms Control*, pp. 95–97.

violation in the case at hand (particularly how much cheating has occurred, over how long a period, in what ways, and by means of what deception), the more sensible and justifiable may be that nation's response to the violation. Thus, if the general pattern of compliance has been good and the specific violation was short-lived and could be prevented in the future, a gross or violent response would be out of place. But if the information system has not functioned well enough to provide such information, the nation will have to make the political-military decisions about continuation and response without the benefit of such potentially reassuring or disquieting information. Both the agreement and its parties may be the losers.[12]

The "missile gap" of the early 1960s serves as an interesting instance of inadequate information and its consequences. The United States and the Soviet Union had what could be viewed as a tacit agreement not to speed up the production and deployment of ICBMs. At the beginning of the 1960s, however, American intelligence reported that the Soviets would soon gain a monstrous deployment superiority. Consequently, the United States, under the initiative of the new Kennedy administration, markedly increased its projections and production of American ICBMs. The result was a massive American superiority that still persists, for it developed that American intelligence had made the frequent military error of deducing intentions from capabilities and so attributed to the Soviets plans they did not have. Had the information system been better, the American race to massive superiority could not have been justified in such terms of reciprocation.

It must be recognized that any information system, particularly the verification and inspection provisions of arms control agreements, will have its limitations. No information system is perfect. But none need be. The system may be designed to uncover all violations, or only the grosser ones. It may be constructed to provide information that will convince one nation that another has cheated, or to provide information sufficient to persuade arms control organs and the other nations that a violation has occurred. This distinction between adequacy for knowledge and adequacy for persuasion could prove important; a nation will supplement the information it receives through the agreement's provisions with its own intelligence sources, but it may not be desirous of revealing this supplemental or corroboratory information because revelation might betray the source. Moreover, the information

---

[12]Other provisions governing responses to perceived or suspected violations will be considered later in this chapter.

system may be designed to be relevant and adequate at the time of the agreement, but unless the agreement is short-lived or provisions are designed to change with changing technology and developing evasion capabilities, the information provisions, unless supplemented, might become obsolescent after agreement.

In these and other ways, information provisions will be imperfect, because they are either inadequate or simply incomplete. But there are several reasons why they need not be either perfect or complete. First, a participant nation must make decisions on political-military grounds about the degree of completeness and adequacy that the nation will demand. There are several important questions to be considered: What kind, size, or quantity of violation would be irreversible and mortal or otherwise unbearable? How much of a risk of such unbearable consequence would be bearable in view of the costs of obtaining better protection and the best guesses about the risks the others might be prepared to run in violating? What information provisions offer only that much risk of unbearable violation? It is the employment of such calculation and design which governs the acceptability of imperfection.[13]

The limitations of information systems are not confined to coverage. But the more basic technical problems have been quite well handled in the literature on inspection.[14] A few of the important problems are considerations of possibilities and limits technological, human, and financial. The technological problems raised by detection

[13]See Martin C. McGuire, *Secrecy and the Arms Race* (Cambridge, Mass.: Harvard University Press, 1965), for a model and a theoretical analysis of the effects of information on armament and brief application to arms control.

[14]See Seymour Melman (ed.), *Inspection for Disarmament* (New York: Columbia University Press, 1958); the chapters by Sohn and Frisch, Kalkstein, and Phelps in David H. Frisch (ed.), *Arms Reduction: Program and Issues* (New York: Twentieth Century, 1961); the chapter by Wiesner in Louis Henkin (ed.), *Arms Control: Issues for the Public* (Englewood Cliffs, N. J.: Prentice-Hall for the American Assembly, 1961); the chapters by Wiesner, Feld, and Bohn in Brennan (ed.), *Arms Control, Disarmament, and National Security;* the chapters by Bohn, Melman, Gerard, Karl Deutsch, and Schelling in Quincy Wright et al. (eds.), *Preventing World War III: Some Proposals* (New York: Simon & Schuster, 1962); the chapters by Rodberg, Finkelstein, and Sohn in Seymour Melman (ed.), *Disarmament: Its Politics and Economics;* and Lawrence S. Finkelstein, "Arms Inspection," published as *International Conciliation,* no. 540, November (1962). See also the less technical and more strategic approach in Thomas C. Schelling and Morton H. Halperin's *Strategy and Arms Control,* chap. 9; and the analysis by the Institute for Defense Analyses, *Verification and Response in Disarmament Agreements,* The Woods Hole Summer Study 1962, produced under contract with the U.S. Arms Control and Disarmament Agency (Washington, D.C.: Institute for Defense Analyses, 1962).

of possible violation and identification of the instance detected as in fact a violation have received considerable and often ingenious thought, which has resulted in proposals of "inspection by the people" (the use and encouragement of private citizen nationals in the inspection process, as suggested by Seymour Melman), the employment of national law and legitimacy symbols to encourage compliance (as suggested by Roger Fisher and Karl Deutsch), the application of nonphysical inspection instruments, such as the polygraph (as proposed by Seymour Melman, Lewis Bohn, and others), and the use of sampling in the designation of inspectable areas and in the inspection of designated areas (as primarily developed by Louis Sohn).[15]

A limitation not so often recognized is the human one. Inspection and verification will probably require large numbers of generally and specially trained individuals. The long-standing debate over the relative merits of adversary inspection (in which each side inspects the other) and impartial inspection (in which neutral or international civil servants inspect each side)[16] should recognize the fact that qualified inspectors would probably be limited in number and limited in nationality to the major adversaries, who have played "hiders and finders" in developing inspection capabilities. Also, it is mostly the cost of the human and mechanical inspection forces that has led Schelling and others to suspect that substantial arms control could cost even more than whatever savings would be realized by cuts in peacetime military spending.

Another aspect of the technical problems of arms inspection is the factors that determine the reliability of the inspection and verification, such as the extent of the area to be inspected and the number of inspections allowed, the number and type or sensitivity of the facilities where inspection is permitted, the rights of access of the inspectors, and the nature of the obligation of the host country to allow inspection. Analysis has determined the importance and effect of each of these factors and has suggested ways in which each factor can be varied to ensure satisfactory inspection in relation to a specific arms control measure.

In any event, the technological, human, and financial limitations

[15]These and other proposals are presented and analyzed in the articles cited by author in the preceding footnote as comprising the best of the inspection literature.

[16]See Lawrence S. Finkelstein, "Arms Inspection," pp. 64–78; the Institute for Defense Analyses, *Verification and Response in Disarmament Agreements,* annex II, pp. 67–70, 72–84; and Fred C. Ikle, *Alternative Approaches to the International Organization of Disarmament,* pp. 3–11.

on the information process, as well as reliability factors of the process, are dependent upon what is acceptable to the participants. While the Western nations, traditionally "open societies," have generally considered inspection as well as verification with interest rather than alarm, the Soviets have tended to view inspection as intrusion and verification as espionage. In the past, the Soviets have always sought to avoid concessions to external authority, whether adversary or international.[17] Furthermore, in the past, the Soviets accepted disarmament only as a propaganda instrument, because of the Leninist contention that revolution will be achieved by force and arms. However, the development of nuclear weapons has led the Soviets to contend both that nuclear war is too dangerous for either side and concomitantly that communism can triumph by peaceful means. Disarmament would thus be unacceptable if it were again to render war possible for capitalism or necessary for communism. And so, inspection would be unacceptable if it gave capitalism the opportunity to exploit its new-found knowledge of the Soviet military establishment in a first-strike attack. But the mutual development of invulnerable second-strike seaborne forces should render this possibility increasingly improbable, barring major breakthroughs in antisubmarine warfare capabilities. Hence, objective grounds could be found for doctrinal acceptance of inspection should the Soviets further overcome their xenophobia and eventually conclude that disarmament would be politically and militarily desirable and promising.

Even the relatively meaning-free negotiations in Geneva have evidenced progress in the mutual sophistication of the adversaries about the necessary role of information concomitant with the development of new techniques and new devices by analysts and scientists of each side.[18] These developments increasingly suggest that even if general and comprehensive disarmament cannot be satisfactorily verifiable, lesser but substantial measures of arms control probably need not always be stillborn as a result of information trauma.

Nonetheless, detection and identification of violation are not enough to guarantee the acceptability, let alone the longevity, of an arms control

[17]For analyses of Soviet attitudes toward inspection, see Arthur Dean, *Test Ban and Disarmament* (New York: Harper & Row, 1966), chap. 3; Walter F. Hahn, *Internal Motives for Soviet Secrecy* (Washington, D.C.: Institute for Defense Analyses, 1963); and Charles Burton Marshall, "Hide and Seek."

[18]See Sir Michael Wright, *Disarm and Verify: An Explanation of the Central Difficulties and of National Policies* (London: Chatto & Windus, 1964), especially chaps. 9–11; and Arthur Dean, *Test Ban and Disarmament*.

agreement. The more important question, put years ago and still being asked, is—"After detection—what?"[19]

Control

What is often referred to as the "problem of control" in international agreements arises out of compliance and violation and the concatenation of interests, activities, and events that constitute anticipation of and response to such compliance and violation. The effective instruments of argument, promise, threat, exchange, and compulsion will be employed both in preventive regulation and in consequent enforcement under any international agreement with control provisions. These instruments will be applied by various national and transnational bodies or forces to affect the behavior of participant states. While they may be used to impose arms control on a reluctant party or more limitedly to induce participation, the analysis presented here will focus upon their employment to affect the behavior of participants. A better understanding of the nature of this control problem and of its place in arms control provisions and practice will depend upon consideration of who is to control whom in what ways.

Nations appear to share with people what Bertrand de Jouvenel has termed "that capital feature of the 'political animal,' the propensity to comply.[20] This is not to say that nations will always observe commands and fulfill commitments. But it does note that, whether for reasons of individual morality or an institutional resistance to breaking rules,[21] and despite the unimpressive treaty-keeping records shared by many if not most nations,[22] nations may keep agreements when there appears to be little immediate justification for doing so. Nonetheless, the analyst should turn to considerations of national interest when

[19]Fred C. Ikle, "After Detection—What?" *Foreign Affairs,* January (1961), pp. 208–220.

[20]Bertrand de Jouvenel, *The Pure Theory of Politics* (New York: Cambridge University Press, 1963), p. 73.

[21]See Roger Fisher, "Constructing Rules That Affect Governments," in Brennan (ed.), *Arms Control, Disarmament, and National Security,* pp. 56–57.

[22]See the recent *Study "Riposte": Responses to Violations of Arms Control and Disarmament Agreements,* by the Historical Evaluation and Research Organization (HERO) (Washington, D.C.: HERO for the U.S. Arms Control and Disarmament Agency, 1964) for an interesting historical study of violations and responses in international agreements.

estimating the prospect of compliance and the possibility of control in the implementation and maintenance of arms control agreements.

It is quite clear that there will be substantive reasons—reasons arising from the specific arms control provisions of the agreement—for a nation's compliance or violation of an agreement. But there will also be procedural reasons for compliance that are unrelated to the specific arms control provisions. Various considerations may encourage states to comply with agreements, particularly treaties, even under unfavorable conditions and at considerable inconvenience. Any agreement is an episode in a continuing relation, and so a state will have an interest in preserving its international reputation and the value of its word in the eyes of other states—and perhaps also in the eyes of "world opinion"[23] and of its own citizenry—by complying. It may also fear that its violation of one agreement will lead to violation or abrogation by other parties of other agreements it appreciates.

This consideration suggests another: fear of reprisal for violation. Whether or not the agreement provides for the possibility of such controlling actions as reciprocal evasion, abrogation, or restoration of the status quo, response to violation can be quite distasteful for the recipient. However, a nation must expect detection and fear response if such considerations are to weigh seriously upon it. If a violation can be concealed or is believed to be concealable, or if there seems reason to believe that reprisal will not follow detection, rational compliance probably will not be motivated. An important determinant of a nation's susceptibility to such considerations of "procedural" interest is its independence or capacity to resist the control efforts that might be applied by others.[24]

Many arms control advocates have desired general and comprehensive disarmament and have sought to devise control provisions that would be able to protect the weaker states from the greater and to prohibit the greater states from quarreling with each other. Some would argue that an international army, with or without a concomitant world government, would permit such success; but the burden of demonstration must remain with such advocates. On the other hand, it is not

[23]For the difficulties of such conceptions, particularly their limitations as effective control considerations, see Fred C. Ikle's article "After Detection—What?" and HERO's Study "Riposte," annex III-A.

[24]Thus, states will vary in ability to resist the imposition of control provisions. The nature of the control provision to be applied must be taken into account in assessing rank independence. See the discussion of interdependence later in this chapter.

difficult to believe that a harmonious condominium of superpowers could impose its arms-controlling will upon most other nations, although it remains difficult to believe that such a condominium will arise. In any event, it should be recognized that strictly controlling the greatest powers, in anything but the disarmed world which seems unreachable, would be a task beyond the capabilities of the control provisions to be considered here.

This suggests that distinctions should be made among nations in terms of both their independence and capacity to resist control as well as their interest in the arms control agreement in question. A nation may be anywhere on the interest continuum from unalterably opposed through reluctant to comply and tempted to violate to unconcerned and (perhaps hence) careless about compliance regardless of motivation and interest.

The controllability of a participant in an agreement is a function of its capacity to resist control and its net interest in noncompliance. A superpower that has become unalterably opposed to the agreement while still quite powerful cannot be controlled, and there seems little hope that in such cases compliance can be brought about. The costs of controlling a middle-range power unalterably opposed to an agreement (such as Gaullist France or Communist China opposing an agreement imposing or strengthening bipolar nuclear control) would be so great that, unless that nation were not a valued member of either major alliance, the necessary efforts at such control would probably be considered unacceptable, if not necessarily impossible. On the other hand, a lesser state unalterably opposed could probably be compelled were other states prepared to pay the costs of imposition. Arms control enforcement will depend upon considerations of the cost of control to the participants, which is a function of the capacity to resist and strength of opposition of the deviant party, and upon the strength of the shared interests in control of other parties to the agreement. Control of a dissident nation becomes manifest in the contributions that the control provisions make to the interest considerations of the participant nations and may be exploited after violation by restoring the status quo or, perhaps, administering punishment. But this will only be possible if the deviant still recognizes a net interest in persistence of the agreement despite suffering such setbacks.

Thus, control provisions should be designed to operate upon major powers who are reluctant to comply (or, as more likely, reluctant to continue complying) or who are otherwise tempted to violate; they should be designed to operate upon nations who are unconcerned and, therefore, inducible either way or who are careless, regardless of motivation, and become responsible for inadvertent, accidental, or unauthorized violations. The provisions might also be designed to operate effectively upon middle-range powers, at least up to cases of reluctance to comply and possibly up to situations of unalterable opposition when the major powers are mutually interested in encouraging compliance. Then, in cases where participation of lesser states becomes important, the provisions should be designed to control them, even where they are unalterably opposed to the arms control agreement.

These propositions do not imply that every agreement ought to be composed of such control provisions. However, these are probably the limits of control provisions. Ingenuity and expense probably should not be lavished upon imagination and construction of what might appear to be ways around these limitations, nor should despair inhibit efforts to design controls that might operate up to these opportunities. If arms control matters enough to the participants, there is reason to believe that control up to these possibilities could be achieved. If circumstances were such that arms control could be forced upon a superpower, despite its unalterable opposition, then there would have been a fundamental change in the international system in the direction of unitary control. Thus, this examination of the problem of control will be concerned with the problem of controlling a major power reluctant to comply with or tempted to violate the arms control agreement.

One analyst has written that "disarmament conferences have failed because they have not and cannot decide the basic political question, the question of who (at the international level) is to coerce whom."[25] Both the nature and the nationality of possible controlling forces may vary.

The most widely imagined international control force is police forces and armies. But there is a useful distinction to be made between "police forces" and "armies." Forces that are employed basically in the *ex ante* regulation of conduct and that attempt to prevent noncompliance by deterrence (threat of apprehension and punishment) and compulsion (preventive interposition or apprehension) could be called "police forces." When forces are employed internationally in *ex post* enforcement of violated regulations and settlements, by restoring the status quo and apprehending the violator, they could be called "armies."

[25]Thornton Read, *Military Policy in a Changing Political Context* (Princeton, N. J.: Center of International Studies, 1961), p. 61.

In addition, there would probably be administrative forces. Some administrative units might be employed to detect evasion and conduct adjudication, but the central control function of administrative forces would be the pronouncement and, if possible, application of sanctions—not only punishments for violation, but also restitution or damages to those injured by violations, and perhaps also rewards for compliance.

Whether police, army, or administrative in nature, the nationality of the control force will be a serious consideration. Control forces might be national. If they are unilateral (and, in the term used to describe inspection forces, "adversary"), they would be yet another manifestation of the most traditional method of control: self-help. But it is also possible that the national forces would be those of a neutral nation, or nations such as the Scandinavian peace-keeping force, which has been constructed for use by the United Nations. Such forces could play an important role in controlling smaller nations—so long as the nations applying such forces remained neutral.

Control might also be undertaken by compound national forces—allied (if alliances persist directed against an adversary or perhaps against a member), condominial (if there are several nations in accord upon the control to be undertaken), or a joint national composition, arising from accepted collective security obligations.

Finally, control might be undertaken by transnational forces, either specially recruited or created out of donated national units and forged into an international force that is, at least in theory, beyond the control of the contributing nations.

It seems probable that because of the likely continuing residence of much sovereignty in the nation states, the nature and composition of control forces, whether administrative, police, or army, would be determined more by political national interests and penchants than by the tasks that such forces would have to undertake. But the undertaking of those tasks of regulation, enforcement, and sanction that arise out of national behavior and out of the provisions of the arms control agreement will help to determine the success or failure of the arms agreement.

There are four stages of control: anticipation, action (compliance or violation), observation, and response. These stages will be continuous and intermeshed in most cases, but they are analytically separable.

The anticipation stage of control is characterized by preventive regulation. The opportunity for such regulation will reside in the interest considerations of a participant nation, and upon them will be played the regulative activities, whether by international forces or by national "self-help" forces. The participant's interest in violation may arise from discontent or fear, causing it to feel "compelled" to cheat by the nature of its situation or by the suspicion (or knowledge) that another is cheating. Such considerations are more apt to occur after an agreement has been in force for some time and the international situation has unexpectedly changed or after another party has had time and interest and success in evading the provisions. Although preventive regulation may succeed in changing interests in and foiling efforts at evasion, over time such interest would suggest that alteration of the world (through such steps as application of "peace-keeping" provisions or procedures for "peaceful change") or of the agreement itself (through amendment or other ways of change) would be more satisfactory to the participant and hence would probably bode better for the persistence of the agreement. These are maintenance provisions and will be considered in Chapter 7.

The participant's interest in violating the agreement may also arise from "greed"—a preference for cheating because of a belief that it will achieve a bonus by doing so. It is this possible basis for evasion that would be best coped with by applying preventive regulation.

The measures of preventive regulation are applications of what have been called above the "instruments of effect": argument, threats and promises, exchange and transfer, and compulsion. *Argument* would take the form of presentation of reasons—perhaps information about expectable consequences of or responses to detected violations and information about the likelihood of detection—designed to change the interest calculations of the participant. Generally, such presentations would be made frequently to any parties to an agreement, perhaps through the obvious presence of observers and enforcers as much as in statements from the administrative organs of the agreement.

The second and third measures of preventive regulation are positive and negative incentives: *threats and promises* and *ex ante exchange and transfer*—intended to deter violation through the promise or payment of goods and the promise and perhaps even the payment of undesirables.

The fourth instrument of preventive regulation is the *observation*, or information, forces themselves, the existence and functioning of which promise revelation and imply further consequence.

The fifth type of measure is *compulsion*—the use of police to force compliance by making noncompliance impossible for or unbearable to the participant, just as the presence of armed guards (if the guard system is efficient and adequate) makes theft unbearable because of its promised concomitants and just as preventive arrest makes commission of crime impossible.

The final means of preventive regulation is *amendment*—the provision for change that can be employed by those unhappy with the existing requirements of the agreement or the existing international order. These are the alteration provisions. This means of regulation is, of course, quite like that of exchange and transfer, but in this case the "goods" involved are opportunities for change rather than materials or deeds themselves.

Besides preventive regulation, there is the possibility of preventive or pre-emptive evasion by another party. The same incentives that would dissuade more "conventional" violation should operate to dissuade such anticipatory violation. But the possibility of preventive violation must not be overlooked. There may be circumstances where the likelihood and danger of other violation would strongly suggest acceptance—with controls—of such anticipatory violation, while ways to alter and strengthen the agreement over time are sought.

The application of preventive regulation in itself may induce or compel compliance. If compliance occurs through inducement, compulsion, or voluntary action motivated by considerations of national interest apart from these anticipatory interventions, then the "cycle" begins again, with anticipation of the behavior of another party or the behavior of the same party in approaching its next obligation. But if violation is not anticipated, if the instruments of preventive regulation are not employed, or if anticipation and regulation fail to induce or compel compliance, the perception or observation of violation (and perhaps the adjudicatory decision that it is indeed a violation that has been detected) will set the stage for response to violation.

Sensible response to violation, whatever the responding organ, will be based upon the nature of the violation. There are important distinctions to be made among violations in terms of their nature, degree, and motivation.

A violation is substantive if it concerns the specific arms control provisions of the agreement; it is procedural if it concerns other aspects, such as verification and inspection or adjudication provisions. In general, the substantive violations will present the clearest immediate threat to the security of the other parties. But because procedural violations may be the result of concealment of substantive violations, they cannot be easily dismissed.

The immediate seriousness of a violation will depend upon its scope and magnitude. Violation of the entire agreement will be more serious than violation of one provision, just as violations of the spirit will probably be of more significance than violations of the letter that remain within the spirit. Here there is a possibility of grave problems of definition and determination, and the role of the adjudicatory body will be crucial. If the adjudicatory organ should become legalistic and pounce upon violations of the letter, while ignoring violations of the spirit of the agreement, the faith of the parties in the agreement and its created organs as acceptable substitutions for parts of the national military establishments will almost certainly decline and the agreement will be jeopardized.

In many instances, however, more important for the survivability of the agreement and probably for the confidence of the participants will be the motivation for, or explanation of, the violation. A violation may be intentional, inadvertent, accidental, incidental to interpretation, or unauthorized. If the violation is unauthorized—committed by an agent in violation of the orders of its national government and the terms of the agreement— it should not be a serious threat to the agreement itself, provided that it is reversible and not itself dangerous to the other parties. If the violation is a result of variant interpretation, it should not be a serious threat to the life of the agreement, again provided that it is neither dangerous nor irreversible and that an adjudicatory body can straighten out conflicting interpretations to the satisfaction of all participants. However, it should be anticipated that a country intent upon violation, once discovered, would contend that it had a variant understanding of the provisions of the agreement. Thus, interpretive violations must be considered important and worthy of careful immediate attention. If the violation is inadvertent (resulting from human error or carelessness) or accidental (resulting from mechanical or other nonhuman error) it should not pose a grave threat to the life of the agreement, again presuming the violation's limited character and its reversibility. In these cases, it would be hoped that the parties would learn from their own and others' violations and that such violations would decrease over time—or, at least, not increase as further arms control provisions became effective.

Somewhere between the inadvertent and the intentional violation will fall the distinction between violation and noncompliance. In many cases, such a distinction would be analytically rather than operationally significant. But while pure violation is active and tends to be quite clear, noncompliance is often passive and unclear, implying inadvertence rather than intentional violation. An important and probably revealing test of the nature of noncompliance will be the response of the violator to allegations or discoveries of noncompliance.

One possibility is that of fraudulently induced violations. A nation desiring to undermine the agreement, to detract attention from other activities, or to exploit sanction provisions might fake a violation, inducing a comparable, self-help-motivated violation by another party, only to subsequently demonstrate that it had not actually violated the agreement. Or a nation might undertake activities not expressly in violation of the agreement but still designed to induce violation by another party. This possible threat to the continuance of the agreement indicates again the importance of providing ways in which the agreement's organs can cope with violations and thus free nations from reliance on self-help and reciprocal violation to preserve their security. This will be of further importance if incentives toward nonviolation will also serve as incentives toward nonresponse to violation and if the agreement will identify certain previously acceptable activities as violations, thereby curtailing the possibilities of self-help redress to violations.

The response to discovered violation, whether it be undertaken by individual parties or by international organs created or empowered by the agreement, would consist of four basic responsive tasks. The first is to terminate the violation. The second is to compensate for the violation, ensuring that the agreement will continue to preserve the security of nonviolating participants against any advantages gained by the violator or against threats posed by the violation itself, and thereby maintaining confidence that the arms control agreement can control international politics acceptably and contribute to the national security of participants successfully. The third task is to restore the status quo or, if that is not possible, to make permanent allowance to compensate nonviolators and prevent the violator from gaining advantage. The final task of response will arise from the decision upon and administration of applicable and desired sanctions, including punishments, rewards, and termination of the agreement.

The nature of the response will be affected by who responds. If the organs created or empowered by the agreement undertake the response, there may be a broader gamut of possible responses because the united resources will exceed those of an individual respondent. But there may be a greater dilution and even weakness of will as a consequence of the problems of unifying a multitude of highly sovereign states behind a single purposive and militant program. If there could be established an international army operating under unified direction, compelling control might be possible. But creation of such an enforcement organ seems unlikely. However, in the absence of such an imperial institution, responsive action will probably be further constrained by the strength of the net desire of the violator to see the agreement persist and to remain a part of it.

But whether undertaken by self-helping individual nations, by alliances, by multinational groupings, or by international organizations, the problems of response to violation are problems of consequent enforcement. In a sense, the first response would probably be revelation of knowledge of violation and notification of displeasure. Such information would probably be announced to other participants and even publicly to the world, unless it were judged that quiet revelation would better serve the security purposes which underlay agreement and would allow quiet negotiation of compliance and other possible responses.

The immediate objective will be termination of the violation. This might be achieved by argument in the form of reasoning about the imminence and consequence of other possible responses that would follow if the violation did not cease.

But other objectives, especially immediate security compensation for nonviolators to restore the balance and to remove the violation at least temporarily, will quickly become dominant in determining the nature of responses. At any time, the instruments of effecting action employed by the respondents can serve several purposes and can be introduced in various progressions and combinations. Analytically, they may be separated into six further types beyond revelation and argument.

Both compulsion and the employment of threat and promise may be directed at termination of the violation as well as at restoration of the status quo. If the agreement persists, compulsion could be effected by the international army (if one exists) or unilaterally by the injured nonviolators if they were prepared to see the agreement disintegrate under such a barrage of self-help. Restoration of the previous situation, an effort to remove the violation permanently, will probably involve the application of traditional diplomatic measures and the employment of promises and threats.

If threats do not bring about compliance, or if promises do, fulfillment of the threat or promise will be appropriate. This movement from conditional statement to its fulfillment will result in action similar to that of another category of effective instruments of response: exchange and transfer. Exchange and transfer refers to that sanction most often suggested but rarely imposed: punishment. However, it should be conceived much more broadly to include rewards as well as punishments.

Punishment and reward are two very similar sanctions, serving the same basic function, having complementary justifying effects, and even being grounded in the same international interdependence. Their basic function is to insure or encourage compliance beyond the intrinsic desire of the party, so that others can have confidence, if not in the party then in the operating agreement.

The justifications that derive from the specific functions of punishment and reward might be found in the theory of legal practice and applied to the analysis of international practice.[26] The most general and perhaps most widely recognized function is that of education, both of the party acted upon and, by example, of others. It is an education of minds through the lessons of deterrence by punishment and of encouragement by reward. Punishment and reward are independent activities—that is, punishing one party does not necessarily reward or bring about the reward of another, although there may be such a tendency to the extent that international relations can be characterized as, in the words of game theory, "a zero-sum game."[27]

A second function of punishment and reward is compensation—for anguish caused, damages imposed, or other suffering resulting from violation. This general function, which serves a similar purpose to temporary compensation for security threats, is manifest in a transfer to the "rewarded" nation generally from the "punished" nation. If the injurer is unable to "pay" (that is, if he is unable to restore security to the nonviolator), social insurance might compensate (that is, organs of the international agreement might restore security somehow).

The third function is another transfer relation: restoration, which is similar to the responsive effort to re-establish the status quo. It will generally be characterized by a removal of advantage from the "punished" party (such as forced disarmament of a fraudulently gained force) and, in the event of reward, a similar repayment to the "rewarded" party (such as permission to improve its position in relation to the violator).

[26]An interesting presentation somewhat similar to this one is that by Glanville Williams in "The Aims of the Law of Tort," in *Current Legal Problems*, vol. 7. (London: Stevens, 1951), pp. 137–176.

[27]That is, a game in which a gain for one side is necessarily a loss for the other, and vice versa. Such a characterization is demonstrated to be inaccurate by the fact that there can be incentive for cooperation in such areas as arms control. More fundamentally, it is rendered inapplicable by the fact that there are not two sides pure and simple, but rather various alliances and alignments characterized internally by both accord and discord.

A fourth function is that of control or compulsion, similar to one termination response to violation, and manifest in incapacitation of the "punished" and strengthening of the "rewarded." In a "zero-sum" confrontation, the one act will concomitantly bring about the other; in a "non-zero-sum" situation, both punishment and reward may be undertaken by an intermediary, such as an arms control organ.

The final function, similar to that of the application of sanctions in the response to violations, is the "gratification" of society at the expense of the wrongdoer. It will be manifest in unilateral penalty explained in terms of "expiation" by the punished and in comparable "receipt" by others, usually of a sense of vengeance in viewing the punishment of the wrongdoer.

Each of these general types of punishment and reward might be applied to participants on the basis of their behavior in an arms control agreement, either by an international organ or by other parties (acting in individual or collective self-help). However, this is an unusual and perhaps questionable proposition, and it should be further examined.

Recent anthropological and sociological research has indicated that provisions for damages and mediation almost always precede the creation of police forces in the primitive world.[28] This discovery could be explained by the need to build cultural foundations in the community before establishment of a regime of confidence-inspiring control becomes possible. Before reasoning by analogy from primitive societies to the "primitive" international order, it would be well to remember that nations are much more powerful, independent, and relatively deficient in common culture and interests than subtribal units. However, nations also have their own domestic systems of mediation, police, and counsel, and hence in that sense are farther along the legal-development path. This suggests that it would be sensible to exploit and rely upon national systems of law, police, and sanction wherever possible in the control of national behavior under an arms control agreement.[29]

[28]See Richard O. Schwartz and James C. Miller, "Legal Evolution and Societal Complexity," *American Journal of Sociology*, 70 (1964), pp. 159–169. See also Roger D. Masters, "World Politics as a Primitive Political System," *World Politics*, 16 (1964), pp. 595–619.

[29]Some measures relying upon domestic law and citizens have been mentioned in the discussion of information provisions above. The use of domestic instruments in enforcement has been suggested and developed by Roger Fisher. See especially his article "Internal Enforcement of International Rules," in Seymour Melman (ed.), *Disarmament: Its Politics and Economics*, pp. 99–120.

A principal difference between a society grounded in a developed legal code and institutions and an underdeveloped society like the international order is the incentive for a member to remain in it and the difficulty of getting out, regardless of the punishment applied. For the very possibility of usefully employing punishment and reward in the service of an international arms control agreement depends upon the continuing desire of the constituents to remain within the agreement, or at least within the broader "legal" control community that would enforce the agreement. This ineluctable fact raises the much presumed but little analyzed problem of the interdependence which creates or nourishes desires to remain constituents of an international arrangement or control community.

As a basis for punishment, interdependence keeps the punished party tied to the agreement, or at least tied to the system, provided that it is reinstated after punishment. As a basis for reward, interdependence makes it possible for one party to help another, because they operate as constituents of a system in which the actions of each will affect the others. The nature of this interdependence is a dependence on one another.

Appreciation of the obvious development of communication and transport and its effects upon military affairs, international trade, international finance, personal relations, and even global values[30] might suggest that interdependence has increased in the twentieth century. But concomitant emphasis upon autarky, or self-sufficiency—especially military, but also financial and economic (in particular, development and diversity)—coupled with the consequences of increasing multipolarity politically and economically, may indeed have decreased fundamental interdependence, at least for the major powers for whom autarky has become an increasing reality.[31]

The basis of interdependence would seem to be a commitment, whether necessary or voluntary, to the system. In this sense, interdependence is like trust[32] and hence results in the creation of opportunities for influence, which becomes a possibility where there have been

[30]See Ernst B. Haas and Allen S. Whiting, *Dynamics of International Relations* (New York: McGraw-Hill, 1956), chap. 1, for a discussion of "the fact of interdependence and its denial."

[31]See the argument by Kenneth N. Waltz in his review article, "Contention and Management in International Relations," *World Politics,* 17 (1965), pp. 735–737, for brief documentation of the case against increasing economic interdependence.

[32]See the discussion of the nature of trust above.

investments in the system. Such influence is manifest in the reward and punishment delivered by the system or its constituent parts to individual members. Therefore, it would appear that the autarkic tendencies manifest by large powers would undermine not just interdependence as such, but also the possibilities for reward and punishment by the international system. But this may not be the case. The presumption is misleading because it overemphasizes the dependence in interdependence. Although the large powers can themselves get along alone in most respects and at least for a time, they also have or adopt interests extending beyond their borders. Thus, the United States encounters other nations resisting Communist inroads abroad; these nations become dependent upon American assistance in resisting; and because the United States needs them for their resistance, they become able to exercise considerable influence upon the United States. Thus, large powers become dependent upon small states, while small states continue to be dependent upon the large powers. Moreover, the important factor is not interdependence, but patterns of interaction, or more specifically transaction, which bring about "interadvantage." The attainment of goods depends upon relations with other members of the system. International intercourse is advantageous, so reward will be appreciated and punishment will hurt if they affect the nature of that intercourse. In other words, continued international intercourse will be desirable, heightened intercourse (reward) will be appreciated, and exclusion from the society (punishment) will be disfavored. If this is the realm of reward and punishment, it is admittedly a marginal realm, at least in the cases of large and relatively autarkic powers. But then, the interesting cases where the maintenance of arms control measures might be affected by reward and punishment are cases where marginal incentive to violate is to be overcome or prevented.

The place of punishments in such circumstances is rather clear. But that of rewards is less clear. It was indicated earlier that many rewards can be viewed as the complements of punishments, because of the transfer nature of the restoration and compensation cases. But further, rewards may be employed to reinforce compliance. As most sanction systems are envisaged, a violator would be punished (assuming he chooses to remain within the agreement or were otherwise subject to punishment) and if possible the violation would be removed. But, particularly if the possible debilitating consequences are substantial or if the possibility of debilitating consequences is great, there would probably be built-in incentive to pre-emptive and even preventive evasion by other parties. And there would be great pressure for reciprocal violation once another nation had been found at fault. This would produce grave danger of a violations race, which would share all the dangers of a "purer" arms race and also serve to destroy what was left of the arms control agreement and with that perhaps the possibility of achieving any future agreements.

This suggests that it would be desirable to build into the agreement rewards for unilateral compliance, which would help to compensate a nation faced by a violator-adversary, while the control provisions that would terminate and eliminate the violation were put into effect. It must be recognized that the possibilities of such reward for unilateral compliance would be limited by the extent to which the authority could prescribe measures that would contribute to the nation's security enough to divert it from self-help violations. Indeed, even if the agreement organ were only to approve or provide for the measures that would be taken in unilateral reciprocation for violation, the sway of the agreement, reeling from the first violation, might be preserved.

In addition, it might be desirable to build periodic rewards into the agreement, so that compliance would be rewarded regularly and compliant behavior would thereby be reinforced, even if there had been no violations. If a nation must decide whether or not to violate the agreement and if the possible loss of its benefits and of the opportunity to make further agreements in the future are not quite enough to turn it from violation, the loss of continuing periodic rewards for compliance might be. And such rewards, if directed at the populace, might be particularly useful in keeping the public (often subject to incitement against such an extending agreement by demagogues, militarists, and publicists) in support of compliance.

What would be the nature of these rewards and punishments? Where would they come from? Clearly in cases where they are "transfers," the goods would be transferred from a violator to the sufferent of the violation or to all compliant nations. If there is a mutually desired "currency" (be it money, grants of access, spheres of influence, natural resources, or something else), the transfer could be easily determined. But it might be desirable in some circumstances to transfer different "currencies" through the central authority, or "bank," so that the aberrant nation would be punished and the compliant nation rewarded independently. Alternately, "payment" might be made in the same "currency" in cases where the interests of the nations were not zero-sum, that is, where the transfer would benefit one more than it would hurt the other or would hurt one more than it would benefit the other.

If it is not transfer but unilateral punishment or reward or both that is to be executed, there are several possibilities. "To insure execution and observance, it was customary at one time to give to important treaties a special sanction by oath, the pledge of securities, the delivery of hostages, or a guarantee."[33] While special oaths are out of favor and have probably now lost any special efficacy they once had, the pledge of securities, such as compliance bonds in escrow and even the exchange of hostages, might again be employed. These are possibilities to be provided for in advance, in effect by the pooling or contribution of resources by participants before compliance is undertaken.

Another possibility is the employment of incentives actually created by the cooperation in the agreement. Thus, certain activities (such as alteration of arms postures or granting of political access to certain areas or even recognition of military-political spheres of influence) could only be undertaken authoritatively by the international organ created by the agreement. Also, funds realized from disposal of abandoned weapons, which might have been transferred to the agency under terms of the agreement, could be dispersed by the agency as rewards to compliant members.

A related possibility is alteration of the terms of implementation of the agreement to penalize noncompliance. Although control provisions might be tinkered with, the most likely aspect for manipulation would be inspection. The verification and inspection requirements might be heightened in response to violation—that is, if the areas, types of installations, or other aspects of the military establishment to be examined increase over time, the rate of that increase might itself be hastened following discovery of a violation. Alternately, the violator might in the future be expected to produce more evidence of compliance than would nonviolators, on the principle that what has been done once might be tried again, so that more adequate information safeguards against surreptitious advantage seeking must be provided. Possibilities such as these, built into the agreement before it is ratified, might provide deterrent as well as penalty benefits to compliers, while punishing violators.

There is also the possibility of reciprocated trade of bargaining assets among the parties if the agreement is limited to a small number of parties. "Bargaining assets" refers to nonvital economic, political, and military possessions and activities, the surrender of which would be valued by an adversary. Thus, the United States might offer closure of

---

[33]Samuel B. Crandall, *Treaties: Their Making and Enforcement,* 2d ed. (Washington, D.C.: John Byrne, 1916), p. 9.

overseas bases and relaxation of the embargo on shipment of strategic materials to the Soviet Union and its satellites. The Soviets might offer increased Western access to smaller cities or at least to areas of small military significance and withdrawal of troops from areas of eastern Europe.

Such a trade of bargaining assets, which would be conditional upon continued compliant behavior, closely resembles another possibility for punishment and reward: unilateral actions by the major powers displeased or pleased, affecting any violator and any complier. Most unilateral negative sanctions are economic and financial, involving restrictions upon exports from and imports to displeasing nations, severance of financial relations, and even severance of transport and communications. Measures such as these would presumably do direct harm to a nation's ability to survive and would also make evident to the populace the fact that the nation was being subjected to sanctions for disapproved behavior. There are also the possibilities of direct military sanctions and assistance to adversaries of the disapproved power. But such sanctions might undermine the peace for which the arms control measures had been undertaken. Furthermore, any sanctions are likely to be distasteful to the applicant as well as the recipient, so such military sanctions are likely to be disfavored and hence subject to the kinds of hesitations and objections that confronted the efforts to apply sanctions to Italy over the Abyssinian affair.[34]

It would be possible for sanctions to be desired and employed as rewards for compliant behavior by a major power able to afford the unilateral cost; indeed, by instituting such rewards, the major power perhaps could induce other major powers to follow suit. Traditional foreign aid can be viewed in such manipulative terms, although such terms do not do justice to the gamut of purposes foreign aid is generally intended

[34]See the analysis, placed in a broader context, in the Royal Institute of International Affairs, *International Sanctions* (New York: Oxford University Press, 1938). A brief international legal analysis of the problem of sanctions can be found in chapter 15 of *The Basis of Obligation in International Law, and Other Papers* by James L. Brierly (New York: Oxford University Press, 1958). For an interesting and rather specific economic analysis concerning sanctions, see "A Note on the Economics of Retaliation," in Thomas Balogh's *Unequal Partners,* Vol. 1: "The Theoretical Framework" (Oxford: Blackwell, 1963), pp. 101–108. Analysis more political and of broader gauge centering upon foreign assistance can be found in George Liska, *The New Statecraft: Foreign Aid in American Foreign Policy* (Chicago: University of Chicago, 1960). Finally, see Morris Bornstein, "Economic Sanctions as Responses to Arms Control Violations," *Journal of Arms Control,* 1 (1963), pp. 203–218.

to serve. Aid to adversaries, such as the American sale of wheat to the Soviet Union, is an example of rewarding cooperative or approved behavior. This indicates again the interrelation of all aspects of policy, suggesting that there may be many opportunities within the confines of nonsecurity policy for a nation to make clear and beneficial to another its appreciation of that nation's compliant, if not pliant, behavior. Such actions represent, in effect, side payments,[35] which are intended to alter or complete the formal "game" in which adversaries are engaged and are the final and broadest type of reward and punishment that can be put to the service of compliance with an arms control agreement—unilaterally by a well-endowed and pleased or fretful nation, if not multilaterally by an arms control organization.

Punishment and reward, which are types of exchange and transfer, are not the only sanctions that might be employed in response to violation. Another possibility is reciprocal violation by the other parties to the agreement. The replication of the other's offense is a type of immediate compensation for the deprivation of security that the compliant parties have experienced. If the violation is in fact replicated almost exactly—that is, if the violator produces an extra fifty missiles, and the compliant nations respond by doing the same—the arms race that would be threatened by such a violation might be somewhat constrained.[36] On the other hand, because military establishments and their contexts and envisioned tasks vary so much from country to country and alliance to alliance, strict replication may be an inadequate response. Indeed, if a nation intends a partial evasion of its commitments, it might strategically select the evasion that would contribute most to its advantage (assuming comparable possibilities of avoiding detection for various evasions). And because a measure will be more advantageous if it is not easily provided against, replication in evasion may be a very inadequate response. Hence, nations are unlikely to limit themselves to mimicry in practice and are even less likely to concert upon such a limitation in advance. Thus, the threat of a rearmament race following the discovery of a significant violation is grave.

Whether or not the agreement itself could survive mere replication, to say nothing of a rearmament race, however limited and brief,

---

[35]See the analysis of the nature of side payments in William H. Riker, *Theory of Political Coalitions* (New Haven, Conn.: Yale University Press, 1962), pp. 108–114.

[36]Compare the analogous reasoning for limited nuclear war, presented by Leo Szilard in "Disarmament and the Problem of Peace," *Bulletin of the Atomic Scientists,* 11 (1955), pp. 297–307.

must remain uncertain. But a major possibility following upon response to violation if not upon violation itself would be suspension or abrogation of the agreement, unless there were some other way of denying the benefits of the agreement to the violator until the violation terminated and response was complete.

A final possible response to violation would be war or other forcible and probably unilateral acts of redress and reprisal, fulfilling the punishment function of sanction, if little else. Other than war, nations might resort to measures such as embargo, demonstration, and pacific blockade.[37] But because each of these measures almost presumes the end of the arms control agreement, such response would be an act of desperation.

Whatever responses to violation are undertaken, consideration will presumably be given to their effects upon the future, to the responses which these responses are likely to elicit. Thus, whether the response is likely to induce recompliance, a rearmament race, or abrogation, will probably be a major consideration. Furthermore, because through such unprecedented activity in such novel circumstances, the parties are writing the rules of the game while playing it, careful attention must be given to the precedents being set, strengthened, or undermined by the response to the violation. The future of further agreement, as well as of further compliance with the present agreement, will depend in large part upon the effectiveness of responses to the initial violations.

It is important to remember, in addition, that responses must be made not only to violation, but also to compliance. Presumably the basic response to compliance will be reciprocal and perhaps further compliance. But if that compliance was induced by promise, the commitment will have to be fulfilled or broken. And if the compliance is valued and perhaps costly, the compliant nation might be rewarded by the international organization or even by other nations in accordance with measures discussed above. The control provisions and measures, structured in a continuous and intermeshed progression from anticipation through compliance and perhaps violation to response and further anticipation, are more likely to achieve their objective of implementation of the arms control agreement if they compose a flexible, graduated, and controlled response system to violations proven or suspected.

If, however, all the control activities in the world or all the control provisions in the agreement should fail to preserve the agreement and

_____

[37]See Albert E. Hindmarsh, *Force in Peace: Force Short of War in International Relations* (Cambridge, Mass.: Harvard University Press, 1933), a somewhat dated and internationally law-oriented book, but nonetheless useful.

the security of its parties in the face of serious violation, the question arises: After breakdown—what? The responses to breakdown would probably depend upon the nature and seriousness of the evasion. Were the violation in some fashion reparable, the arrangement might be reconstructed. A rearmament race would be a likely consequence under any circumstances, although it might be limited in ways suggested above. And self-help reprisals might be expected in some cases. But the gravest possibility would be war, initiated by a nation fearing that the disparity brought about through evasion would become worse over time, or by a nation capitalizing upon its new-found advantage.

The responses to breakdown constitute a subject beyond the scope of this study. Much of the analysis of responses to violation would be applicable to this graver situation. But should a nation find itself quite deceived in a world of comprehensive disarmament, its best response might be nonviolent resistance to long-distance dictation and invasion. The promise of such an unorthodox strategy would not be great, but it might exceed that of conventional resistance with inferior armament.[38]

Extension and Termination

Termination of an agreement need not be by breakdown. The flexibility sought in the control provisions may also be built into the life expectancy of the agreement itself through provisions for extension and termination of the agreement. The original agreement will include provisions for termination, whether they take the form of the implicit *rebus sic stantibus* clause or of explicit mention of a date of expiration. Any agreement so serious as an arms control arrangement will almost certainly make provision for withdrawal, probably with due and specified notice. Thus, Article 4 of the testban treaty states that "This Treaty shall be of unlimited duration"; but it continues:

[38]Such a strategy of nonviolent resistance has frequently been proposed by advocates of unilateral disarmament, but has rarely been developed. In Britain, some proponents of unilateral nuclear disarmament have adopted such proposals made by the late Commander Sir Stephen King-Hall in his *Defence in the Nuclear Age* (London: Gollancz 1958), *Common Sense in Defence* (London: *K-H Services,* 1960), and *Power Politics in the Nuclear Age: A Policy for Britain* (London: Gollancz, 1962). This subject has remained underdeveloped despite the recent interest created by the civil rights movement in America. An interesting collection of readings with citations and a bibliography is Mulford Sibley's *The Quiet Battle* (Garden City, New York: Doubleday [Anchor], 1963).

Each Party shall in exercising its national sovereignty have the right to withdraw from the Treaty if it decides that extraordinary events, related to the subject matter of this Treaty, have jeopardized the supreme interests of its country. It shall give notice of such withdrawal to all other Parties to the Treaty three months in advance.

The agreement might also include provisions for extension beyond termination date, perhaps with opportunity for alteration or reservation being specifically provided at the time of extension, as in the North Atlantic Treaty.

A gloss upon these provisions for extension and termination will undoubtedly be developed over time through statements of the participant nations and particularly by precedential acts. Indeed, termination and extension of an agreement is always a subject of continual national decision, influenced by the considerations of national objectives, costs, and benefits, regardless of the specific provisions in the agreement. And thus, termination and extension and the decisions underlying much behavior can be viewed as themselves responses to violation and compliance and so are particularly important aspects, with administration, adjudication, information, and control, of the implementation of arms control agreements.

On the basis of this analysis it *can* be concluded that implementation itself *need* not be a grave problem if the machinery and procedures are well conceived, well established, and well executed. But almost immediately the participants and their international organs are likely to meet unforeseen difficulties requiring adjustment and innovation for the maintenance of the agreement.

CHAPTER 7

The Maintenance
of Arms Control

If even the implementation provisions analyzed in Chapter 6—administration, adjudication, information, extension and termination, and particularly control—adequately cope with internal strain upon an arms control agreement, external stress will almost certainly develop and will tend to alter the agreement as problems that were unforeseen or that could not previously be provided against arise from changes in the environment or in interests and perhaps from malfunctioning of the agreement. Such external stress, while it may be produced by the participating nations, is not intentional in the way that conscious efforts to warp the agreement and its implementation are. These external stresses are provided for in a general way in the agreement by the maintenance provisions for subsequent accession, resolution, elaboration and specification, and alteration. Basically, these provisions will require adjustment of behavior in the parties and innovation of forms in the agreement.

Accession

Perhaps the first external stress that major arms control agreement may encounter will be the challenge of certain nations that are important to the effective functioning and progression of the agreement but that were not original signatories. For example, some nations would become important or even essential to the agreement because of their location and consequent need for inspection, as would be necessary with Canada and Communist China were the United States and the Soviet Union to undertake substantial disarmament. Other nations might become essential because they were needed for service in the administrative, adjudicative, inspection, or control forces. But, more significantly, some nations would become essential because the major parties, signatories from the outset, would be reaching levels and types of control and reduction where the nature and activity of previously inferior and impotent forces could become effective if not similarly controlled and reduced.

Just as an agreement might be constructed in stages to which nations could adhere at will, perhaps making their adherence conditional upon subsequent adherence by others, so an agreement could be constructed to allow other nations to adhere later, either when they awoke to their interests (if they were laggards) or when the provisions began to apply to them (if they were weaklings). Such an open-sided agreement might even allow these others to adhere to as much of the agreement as they pleased when they pleased, at least within limits that provided security for other adherents.

Prospects for arms control would be considerably brighter were there grounds to suspect that all significant nations would adhere when the appropriate time came. However, because the agreement would be constructed to constrain and possibly curtail military establishments, there could be a perceptible advantage in remaining outside the agreement while one's competitors or superiors enter. This raises the very important question of coercive adhesion and membership. The major powers would undoubtedly exert considerable influence upon their allies and even upon the uncommitted to join eventually. But the superpowers would have to be careful that the controls and reductions they themselves submitted to would not weaken them enough to curtail seriously their capacity to encourage others to join. If the agreement worked well at its upper levels and early stages, its economic benefits and even its political benefits might entice some to join and thereby forego the possible benefits of "bandit gains" at the expense of participating members. Reluctant nations might be encouraged also by employment of whatever control forces the agreement created, by conjoined individual applications of sanctions, and even by partial disarmament by the participants at the explosive expense of recalcitrant nonmembers. But whatever provisions were made for subsequent accession, and whatever preparations were made for encouragement of the dilatory and the disinterested, subsequent accession itself could prove an immediate and very serious external stress upon an agreement.

Resolution

When adjudication was discussed in Chapter 6, it was indicated that maintenance of the agreement would probably require a less legalistic and less procedural organ for settlement of disputes that were fundamentally political. Such a body's performance would be comparable to arbitration, conciliation, or perhaps even mediation or good offices, rather than adjudication. It would be an extralegal interpretive and expansive body, applying primarily its own discretion rather than international law or precedent in cases where the parties would still prefer any such kind of settlement to none and where the dispute could not be resolved by adjudication. Advance distinction between cases subject to adjudication and those subject to resolution would probably often be difficult to make and maintain; but, when the will to settle exists, the importance of having an organ able to nonlegally settle important political disputes will probably justify the pain and cost, as well as the possible duplication.

Elaboration and Specification

Agreements about major political matters will almost certainly be incomplete when drafted and accepted, probably for reasons of both necessity and choice. Any significant situation will be so complex that it will be difficult to incorporate even the extent of agreement among the parties. Therefore, the text of an arms control agreement is likely to be elliptical—that is, it will probably omit some relevant things. Furthermore, any agreement will confront an uncertain future, so the parties will find it difficult to construct and incorporate provisions that will of themselves provide clear and acceptable terms for future behavior. Thus, the text is likely to be somewhat general (at a high level of abstraction) and ambiguous (containing some conflict in meanings) as well as elliptical in its description of future circumstances and activities. The important consideration must be, not that the agreement is elliptical, but rather what is being elided: the unforeseeable, the residual difficulty (following agreement in principle and in general practice), or the residual disagreement.

The incompleteness of an agreement may well be by choice. The tactic of deferring difficult problems may be adopted in the belief that half an agreement is better than none. Such agreement may permit containment of disagreement by specification or implication, while preventively quarantining the achievable agreement and working with it. In addition, the consequences of the partial agreement may be valued although incomplete, or the partial agreement may be valued for nonsubstantive hidden or symbolic values deriving from its very existence as an agreement. It is also possible that half an agreement would contribute to attainment of the other half. It should be remembered that as a substantial agreement is implemented, the political context changes. There might then be a possibility of disappearance or alteration of the existing conflicts of action and judgment born of a world characterized by little if any formal agreement. Or there might be the possibility of resolving residual disagreement in a broader settlement. Alternately, parties might seek to engender creative innovation of forms, terms, and other elements to be employed in further agreement. And finally there might be hope of eventual solution by subsequent serendipity.

A "partial" agreement reached on the basis of such considerations might specify residual disagreement through a modus vivendi,[1] through provisions for future or continuous negotiation, or perhaps even through agreement to disagree (as might occur in an agreement between the United States and the Soviet Union specifying that such disagreement be enacted or conducted through or within the rules of "peaceful coexistence"). The agreement might alternatively imply disagreement through extensive ellipsis or by its tacit or informal nature. But the agreement might also attempt to cover up residual disagreement with equivocal or ambiguous language.

The employment of ellipticity, generality, and even ambiguity may be very sensible if it is conscious and if there is reason to believe that time and change will solve problems. But if not, such usage may threaten both the life of the agreement and the well-being of parties naive enough to have signed the agreement. In such situations, the prospect for agreements in general may suffer to the eventual detriment of all. Viewing the proliferation of vague and visionary treaties in this century, Charles De Visscher wrote:

The treaty is the most powerful instrument of change in international relations; to abuse it is to risk losing its moral authority and to jeopardize what is most fundamental in the international order, faith in the given word. The spirit that accounts for this rapid accumulation of international instruments

[1]Samuel B. Crandall, *Treaties: Their Making and Enforcement*, 2d ed. (Washington, D.C.: John Byrne, 1916), p. 7.

is antihistorical and inclined to attribute creative virtue to mere expressions of intent. Nothing is gained by doing violence to facts.[2]

Agreements will necessarily be elliptical and general, if not ambiguous, and will require elaboration and specification over time and through progress. In a sense, such elaboration and specification can be viewed as continual negotiation (carried on in some cases more by deed than by word) within the guidelines of the agreement. But it is a negotiation that is much more flexible and less legalistic than that which might result during adjudication and resolution. Indeed, it may well have been brought about by efforts to avoid provisions likely to create controversy requiring adjudication. Such elaboration and specification will probably be more like *de facto* amendment or alteration.

Alteration

Those constructing and analyzing arms control agreements must recognize not only that much change will almost certainly pose serious challenges to international arrangements over time, but also that international agreements with strong political and military components will have to cope with such change. Not all change will be destabilizing or threatening to the agreement. Indeed, the continued development of rules for living together could contribute considerably to peaceful change and international stability. But most change will be upsetting. Recommendations that are coupled with general expressions of hope for peaceful settlement, such as in the recent American draft disarmament treaties,[3] are quite inadequate in their excessive emphasis upon peacefulness and in their traditional lack of specificity.

One solution to the problem of change is world government; another solution is empire. But such propositions are too futuristic, impractical, and even perhaps distasteful. Whether nations can gradually construct a world rule of law and institutions is a matter of considerable uncertainty. Hence, the possibility of developing, maintaining, and also controlling an international army must be set aside, for it could not be practicable before considerable troubled waters have run over the dam and over the floodgates as well.

[2]Charles De Visscher, *Theory and Reality in Public International Law* (Princeton, N. J.: Princeton University Press, 1957), pp. 116–117.

[3]See the study, *The Peace-Keeping Proposals* (Washington, D.C.: 1964), undertaken by the Washington Center of Foreign Policy Research for the United States Arms Control and Disarmament Agency.

It might be possible to combine reliance upon national police forces to keep order internally within constituents with the employment of an international force thereby freed to operate in controlling compliance rather than controlling conflict.[4] But this would necessitate acceptance of the status quo by the parties to the agreement—and the status quo will be always changing and can be manipulated by any nation that is not a party to the agreement and hence is unlikely to be subject to whatever constraints on intervention are adopted. Consequently, justice and tradition would suffer.

As Henry Kissinger has written,

As the risks of war have become more cataclysmic, the result has not been a universal reconciliation but a perpetuation of all disputes. Much as we may deplore it, most major historical changes have been brought about to a greater or lesser degree by the threat or the use of force. Our age faces the paradoxical problem that because the violence of war has grown out of all proportion to the objectives to be achieved, no issue has been resolved.[5]

Untrammelled change is one type of resolution, and one which might rapidly become dominant in a world of comprehensively and strictly controlled arms.

In some ways, the same stages of control applied to arms control provisions might be applied to the international change that threatens the political bases and underlying stability of the arms control. But unless the arms control agreement includes massive provisions for peace keeping and specifications of change to be constrained, regulation of violation will generally be quite different from regulation of most of the activities and events, such as insurrection and infiltration, which are the causes of much of the turmoil and trouble in the world today. There will be deceptive similarities. The prime distinction between allowable change and violation will be difficult. The peace keeping, like control of violation, will generally be preventive, but it will be directed primarily at the "third world" rather than at threatening major adversaries. And like arms control violation, change will be a unilateral alteration, but an alteration of the world rather than of the agreement.

These considerations do not demonstrate conclusively that peace

⁴This possibility is advocated by Walter Millis in chapter 7 of his book, *An End to Arms* (New York: Atheneum, 1965).

⁵Henry A. Kissinger, *Necessity for Choice* (Garden City, New York: Doubleday [Anchor], 1962), p. 176.

keeping and stable change cannot replace subversion and revolution. But just as consolidation and stabilization of the peace call for accommodation as well as deterrence, so the effective control of national military establishments will call for modification as well as control. National behavior must be modified and that modification encouraged by control provisions and watched over by instruments of information. But, too, the agreement itself must be modified, or at least modifiable— probably in ways less formal and less unanimous than treaty amendment[6] through employment and exploitation of ellipsis and generality followed by elaboration and specification and through the application of convention and circumstance. Perhaps that agreement is best which alters when it alteration finds.

It must be remembered that from each national viewpoint the problem is not one of maintaining the agreement, least of all maintaining unchanged an agreement negotiated under circumstances that could not persist by men who could not foresee perfectly the developing ways of the world. From each national point of view, the problem is maintaining and, if possible, increasing the national security and related goals that the agreement is intended to serve, while seeing that the maintained agreement does not eclipse other national goals, such as economic development and political independence. Thus, it will probably be found desirable that the negotiators of the agreement be succeeded by a continuing committee to oversee, decide upon, and perhaps even bring about implementation of the maintenance activities arising from the agreement, as well as to undertake *de facto* alteration of provisions in cases of subordinate stalemate or further concord.[7]

Both international change and alteration of an agreement in the face of change may prove important in the maintenance of an arms control agreement. Indeed, it will probably be found that the international order, like man and society, will develop and function best when it is characterized by the necessary and meritorious imbalance which will allow and even encourage creativeness, leadership, and achievement. If it is true that "the coherence of a society is thus not just an 'equilibrium' secured by the automatic coming into opposition of coun-

---

[6]See the brief discussion in Louis Sohn's article, "Adjudication and Enforcement in Arms Control," in Brennan (ed.), *Arms Control, Disarmament, and National Security* (New York: Braziller, 1961), pp. 371–373.

[7]See Fred C. Ikle, *Alternative Approaches to the International Organization of Disarmament* (Santa Monica, Calif.: RAND Corporation, 1961), p. 15, for a brief suggestion of such a "standing group" to work out minor details within the framework of the agreement.

tervailing tendencies; it is something more precarious, always needing to be renewed by efforts of will and imagination,"[8] it is true too of the international order. Opportunities and prospects for arms control will result not only from the nature of national plans and actions in the international system, but also from careful delineation of change and its exploitation, which will permit the nations to confront the international system with innovation of ideas as well as procedures, norms as well as forms.

[8]Dorothy Emmet, *Function, Purpose, and Powers* (London: Macmillan, 1958), p. 294.

PART III

The Future
of Arms Control

CHAPTER 8

The Future of National
Arms Control Policies

To know whether nations will control their arms in the coming decade, it must be asked, first, will nations seek arms control individually—that is, will their plans and actions include a quest for arms control? And second, will nations find arms control collectively—that is, will their national actions bring about arms control outcomes. An attempt at a confident answer to these questions must involve prediction. But prediction must be both cautious and explicit. Because our predictive capabilities are limited by the paucity of tested international political theory, we must improvise by projecting the major determinants (or more accurately the major tendency variables) of national policy and action for arms control, which we have already analyzed.

National political conditions have been examined in terms of personalities, roles, governmental structure and operation, and nongovernmental aspects. A general consistency can be expected in personal characteristics of leaders of the major powers and perhaps even of Communist China. Recent successions in the United States, the Soviet Union, and the United Kingdom have provided corroboration for the previously suspect contention that personal idiosyncrasies of leadership are not likely to be of great distinctive significance in international politics. If this is true, then attention can be concentrated upon likely changes in other key variables or factors. The analysis in the preceding chapters suggests that an interest in arms control will depend in part upon the leadership's attitude toward cooperation with the adversary. America's increasing recognition of the importance of understanding and cooperating with adversaries was proclaimed in President Kennedy's "strategy of peace" address at American University, June 10, 1963; this recognition was institutionalized in the subsequent hotline and nuclear testban agreements and further developed with the

reappraisal of NATO and China policy. And there have been concomitant expressions by Soviet leaders. The analyst would be confident in
his prediction that this trend will continue, both because it is hard to
stifle such consideration once it has been begun and because it is likely
to become both habitual and clearly useful. The trend toward greater
willingness to cooperate with adversaries may well be heightened by
lesson learning on both sides from the Vietnam imbroglio in which
neither superpower has been able to gain and which might have been
averted or at least significantly dampened if the parties had cooperated
earlier.

The major role considerations in national politics will continue to
be questions of resource allocation and security provision. There is little
reason to expect the combined military and space effort of the superpowers to decrease in the decade ahead. If even military spending
should decline (perhaps as a consequence of arms control arrangements), it seems highly probable that the space race will absorb any
savings. It must be remembered, however, in assessing the impact of
continuing expansion of governmental military and space spending,
that the economies of both superpowers continue to grow rapidly, and
hence the allocation strains will be moderate unless domestic spending
for great societies, land defloration, and even great leaps forward
should outstrip available resources.

Although national governments will continue to provide military
security, they may be increasingly subject to several influences. The
expansion of military and space efforts will tend to aggrandize the
positions of the military and industry in determination of national
policy and action. However, the concomitant development of cost-
effectiveness analysis, program budgeting, and other such control and
efficiency devices—apparently now being adopted by the Soviets as
well as by the United States—may counter or at least cushion this
increase in role by lessening the economic impact of such spending and
by maintaining or extending civilian governmental control over both
actual spending and program decisions. On the other hand, further
international instability—a foreseeable consequence of significant nuclear proliferation—may compound the military's role as governmen-
tally provided security deteriorates. It is obviously very difficult to
predict these effects, dependent as they are upon national politics as
well as upon international developments. But the only significant
change in role determinants of attitudes toward arms control that seems
likely is a gradual increase in the authority of what Eisenhower warned

against as the "military-industrial complex," which may take the form of a limited discouragement of national interest in arms control.

National political objectives of many nations seem increasingly amenable to arms control. The mounting stockpiles of the superpowers, the likelihood and danger of nuclear proliferation, and the continuing and perhaps increasing political instability in much of the "third world" should encourage many different nations to be interested in arms control. Finally, among national political determinants, public opinion among the major powers and industrialization among others should stimulate interest in arms control. A shift toward realism in Western public opinion can be seen in changing attitudes toward Communist China, in continued uncertainty about American involvement in the war in Vietnam, and in increasing desire to avoid the dangers of multiplying wars in the "third world." This shift may bring increasing interest in arms control. Similarly, increasing (and perhaps significantly, in countries where the public plays a role, *slowly* increasing) industrialization should produce greater interest in military as well as political stability, which will allow focus of interest and energy internally. Thus, national political conditions in most types of states—with the possible exceptions of Communist China and, at least for the present, France—should bring increased interest in arms control measures as aids in the attainment of internal political objectives.

If this is true, the important question becomes whether national material and external conditions will contribute to this developing interest. Our analysis in Chapter 2 indicated that while there appears to be no absolute limit to economic resources—at least for the major powers—available for armament, there will always be a question of allocation in which costs must be weighed. These questions, while basically political, will have major economic aspects, particularly for second-rank nuclear powers, such as France and Communist China, and for second-rank conventional powers engaged in local arms races. It would appear that the desires of managers and planners to maintain economic stability and even growth will increasingly encourage nations—particularly those other than the superpowers—to interest themselves in arms control.

Technology is a variable that can be projected in terms of trends by national rank and is somewhat foreseeable because of the lag that occurs as science is turned into technology. The major areas in which the superpowers may make significant progress in the coming decade include multiple-warhead missiles, civil defense, antiballistic-missile defense, antisubmarine warfare, and space militarization. It is not clear what progress may be made on these programs and hence what their impact upon international military relations will be; but it is clear that each offers significant arms control possibilities and attractions. The cases of the would-be major powers, France and Communist China, are somewhat different, for they can anticipate immediate gains in technological competence—retracing steps of the superpowers—but declining marginal benefits from technological development—and, presumably, increasing marginal attractiveness of arms control. There are many nations with the technological potential for becoming nuclear or, at least, becoming considerably more conventional should they desire such achievement enough to pay the economic price.

These brief remarks about technology only re-emphasize the inextricability of technology and armament. The possibility that armament itself will encourage conflict between the superpowers through accident, misinformation, or miscalculation seems increasingly unlikely as national and international command, control, and communication continue to be improved. As these conditions improve, the contribution of such fears to national desires for arms control will decline. However, there is burgeoning danger that nuclear proliferation may grossly increase the danger of nuclear activity. For the command, control, and communication systems developed by the superpowers are very expensive and require great technological sophistication. New nuclear nations, having just utilized all resources to become nuclear, are unlikely to be able—or willing—to undertake these major programs. Hence, the possibility that arms control measures will increase such data sharing and capability sharing may prove interesting to all nations.

Arms races of various types seem likely and will influence national calculations. Because of the technological plateau reached by the superpowers, arms racing among these nations will probably continue to be largely quantitative. Because quantitative arms races are generally expensive and mutually defeating, the superpowers should be increasingly interested in some high-level arms control apart from the activities and interests of other nations, none of which can expect to approach the military capabilities of the superpowers in the coming decade. Arms races among the middle-range powers are apt to be qualitative, as some seek to follow in the nuclear footsteps of the superpowers, while others retrench conventionally. Among the weakling nations, however, arms races appear both most probable and most destabilizing, for they will tend to be quantitative and to induce assistance from major powers. This consideration should encourage all but the most revolutionary and least self-protective nations to consider possible measures designed to control arms races in the "third world."

Finally, should war come, the likelihood that armament will bring about unmitigated disaster increases as military establishments increase and capabilities proliferate. The only potentially significant curtailment of such dangers of destructive outcome would be arms control measures designed to alter the strategy and deployment of major powers in order to save cities, coupled with continued improvement and diffusion of command, control, and communication capabilities. These should be of particular interest to the major powers.

It is again clear from this examination of national material considerations that international or external conditions continually intrude. So we must begin our examination of the external political determinants of national attitude with a brief description of the international order that has developed in the postwar years and predict how it will evolve in the coming decade.

The basic bipolar confrontation between the United States and the Soviet Union is rooted in both geopolitics and ideology. Technology has, in an important sense, divorced the confrontation from these bases and permuted it into one more psychological than material. Thus, national security was long envisaged as the defense of the state and its peoples through repulsion of invaders and even through deterrence of invasion by demonstrable impermeability. But developments in the technology of destruction and transportation have rendered all territories vulnerable to destruction and so have forced a redefinition of security in terms of deterrence of destruction by credible threat of counterdestructions. Because major war has thus become so unacceptable, secondary national interests, such as inward pleasure (freedom and welfare domestically) and outward pleasure (friendly, helpful, and ideologically compatible regimes externally) have become more important because they are the only acceptable sources of national security increments. At the same time, such national interests have become less attainable because the traditional instruments (the threat and the use of force) can no longer be so easily employed.

This shift from war and defense to deterrence and retaliation has rendered strategy more important and more immediate: The major powers have been forced to cope with their problems and seek their objectives through employment of strategy, which has become fundamentally declaratory rather than operational. The emphasis upon psychological rather than material elements has encouraged characterization of the stalemate that has evolved from the confrontation as a "balance of terror," in which the massive American intercontinental nuclear superiority is offset by a Soviet capacity that holds Europe hostage.[1] But, as has been shown in earlier chapters, there are dangers inherent in such a balance of terror—dangers arising from the possibility of accident or miscalculation and those arising from competitive development of nuclear devices, missiles, and defensive programs, such as the ABM (antiballistic missile), and ASW (antisubmarine warfare), and civil defense.

Some analysts predict that the strategic stalemate will bring disarmament down to less destructive levels and arms control toward less threatening and uncertain military establishments. But the Soviet-American confrontation cannot be examined merely at the strategic nuclear level. The fact that Soviet strategy is largely based upon holding Europe hostage raises the very important concomitant aspect of this confrontation. The American long-range nuclear superiority was developed basically to permit deterrent "defense" of more than the homeland. But before the American intercontinental nuclear capability was believed adequate and before the Soviets could pose a countering nuclear capability, the Western nations developed the North Atlantic Treaty Organization to pose a conventional obstacle to the Soviet conventional forces present and superior in Eastern Europe. When NATO conventional forces failed to reach desired and projected levels, the United States, grossly overcalculating the strength of the Soviet force, developed what came to be referred to as a "counterforce first-strike capability"—the capacity to launch a first strike against the Soviet Union that would effectively disarm the enemy. But, eventually, Soviet nuclear weapon production and missile development rendered that strategy impracticable and encouraged increasing emphasis upon the limitation of any nuclear encounter in Europe or the homelands of the superpowers. Both the doctrines of limited strategic war and the more fundamental American capability for flexible and measured response arose basically as efforts to keep credible the American threat of nuclear involvement in a war which might develop between the Soviets and Western Europe.

The superpower stalemate, through the balance of terror, effectively eliminated politics from the confrontation of American and Soviet homelands. And over time, the political encounters in Europe,

[1]See Philip Windsor's "Western Europe in Soviet Strategy," Adelphi Paper, no. 8 (London: Institute for Strategic Studies, 1964) and the more technical study by Neville Brown, *Nuclear War: The Impending Strategic Deadlock* (New York: Praeger, 1965).

centering around Berlin and the German question but arising also in the Soviet eastern European satellites, came to be manifest largely in strategy and deployment rather than in maneuver of the sort that occurred in the Berlin blockade. Thus, there developed a recognized balance of power in Europe, a balance more like traditional balances of power than the balance of terror between the superpowers.

This European balance of power, existing under the nuclear umbrella of the superpower balance of terror, allowed an increasing return to more traditional political activity. The economic resurgence and Charles de Gaulle's solitary willingness to lead in Western Europe brought about further French emphasis upon development (begun under the Fourth Republic) of a French nuclear capability and encouraged an increase in French political attention to her former colonies, particularly in Asia. The product of French political independence was disarray in the Atlantic Alliance coupled with increased interest in a European settlement on the part of those who believed that such settlement would strengthen European independence and security, along with those who believed it would lessen the risk of major war.

But the stability that is apparent in Europe and in the superpower balance has not come to characterize the rest of the world. What stability there is in world politics is the consequence of a "balance of imbalances."[2] Thus, the persistent United States lead over the Soviet Union in intercontinental strategic delivery capacity is balanced by the Soviet advantage in continental strategic weapons (both manned bombers and nuclear missiles) in Europe. In ground forces, NATO has a general superiority of regular forces over Warsaw Pact powers by about one million, but forces in Central Europe are about equal. NATO's tactical air and small nuclear weapons are superior, but NATO lags in armored vehicles including tanks, and its mobilization capacity is weaker.

Outside Europe and beyond most of the Middle East and Africa (in both of which areas former colonial powers Britain and France maintain considerable capabilities), the United States seems to have a general military advantage when various local military balances are compared. General Allied superiority derives from supremacy at sea and considerable advantages in the capacity to employ air transport and striking power over long distances. Thus, the great Asian offshore islands of Japan, Taiwan, the Philippines, and Indonesia are in the American sphere of competence. And Allied assistance could probably

[2]I owe both this term and much of its development here to James E. King.

permit India, Pakistan, and possibly Thailand to mount forces superior in capability if not necessarily in number to those that the Communist powers could deploy against them. However, there are two categories of peripheral areas in which the Western powers are at clear disadvantage. The first includes those areas in which Soviet forces would be locally decisive: Finland, Iran, and Afghanistan. The second includes areas in which the balance is unclear and where postwar conflict has generally occurred, but where Chinese Communist forces would probably have increasing advantage: Korea, South Vietnam, Laos, Burma, and possibly Cambodia.

It is within this comprehensive balance of imbalance that order develops and orders change. But the balance must be assessed in political as well as military terms. In Asia, American nuclear threats (exemplified by John Foster Dulles's threat of "massive retaliation" delivered to the Communist Chinese) have tended to give way to conventional threats and counterinsurgency activity—notably in Laos and Thailand as well as South Vietnam. Unless the United States should opt for a massive strike at the Chinese mainland, it would seem that this tendency will increase as Communist China pursues nuclear power and concomitantly heightens the disarray in the Sino-Soviet alliance. Chinese growth and independence will increase the problems of providing for local defense in India and Japan and, perhaps, of providing against local aggression by China's allies.

The development of nuclear capabilities in France and China marks a change in forces and their balance, a change that many have opposed as destabilizing. But the gravest dangers at present and in the near future clearly arise in "third world," for the effective military dangers or risks of war and bad relations have tended to shift from threats of confrontation between major powers to local instabilities prompting intervention by major powers. This intervention has begun to take the form of unilateral assistance in weapons and training, and then, occasionally, combat. As long as it is generally accepted by the major powers that intervention is to remain unilateral, pre-emptive intervention will be a dangerous possibility in any unstable area where more than one major power may be concerned. Eventually, the pattern of unilateral intervention is likely to be challenged and the confrontation of major powers in such circumstances, which would likely begin at low levels of involvement, is likely to escalate and thereby to increase instability.

The superpower balance of terror has encouraged some to advocate a quest for disarmament to take advantage of and strengthen the underlying stalemate; others have emphasized the importance of agreement upon strategies of nuclear activity that would spare populations. The European balance of power has encouraged some to hope for a political settlement that would include disengagement and other measures of disarmament; others emphasize the importance of agreement upon strategies that would delay resort to nuclear weapons in conflict. Similarly, the developing instabilities in the "third. world" have encouraged many to seek ways of limiting the destruction of order, which is implicit in such instabilities, and ways of controlling military activity in those areas. The primary resort of such advocates is to proposals of agreements among the major powers not to disseminate information, materials, or weapons that would hasten the day when nuclear weapons become prominent in Asian, African, Mideastern, and Latin American politics, and global agreements by potential recipients not to seek or accept such weapons. But another proposition has been for recognition and observance and even legislation of restraints that would lessen the likelihood that local wars would escalate in weaponry or participation.

These various propositions of arms controls have met with slight success. The more significant arms control proposals undertaken thus far in the postwar period have been confined in their impact to the superpowers: the hotline, the limited nuclear testban treaty, and the ban on orbiting nuclear weapons. That these agreements took so long to reach confirms the suspicion that long periods of gestation, coupled with fear, are required for nations to reconcile themselves to measures of arms control. If this tendency persists, the prospects for arms control—and indeed even the circumstances in which arms control might be recommended and undertaken—will reside not so much in the present international order as in the projection of trends toward the future development of that international order.

As has been suggested above, there seems no reason to believe that the strategic bipolar stalemate will itself alter substantially in the next decade. It is likely, however, that this stalemate will extend decreasingly to the major allies of the superpowers: France and her European allies (or vassals), and Communist China. If the major alliances should degenerate into alignments, as seems likely, there should be more flexibility in European politics and Asian military affairs, marked perhaps by various changes in the oligarchic ranks.

The deterioration of alliances will probably be a consequence more of the internal policies of the significant powers than of geopolitical "necessity." Thus, Gaullism or a succeeding broader Europeanism can be seen as an expression of resentment at all continued political subservience of an economically resurgent Western Europe rather than as a reflection of the historic tendency for Western Europe to play Eastern Europe against the center (Germany) or to play China against Eastern Europe. And the attitude of China can be viewed more as the product of internal development strains and ideological posturing than as the consequence of an inevitable rivalry between the Eastern Pacific and the Western Pacific. Nonetheless, the material bases for these ideological and internal political positions should not be overlooked. It is important to realize that these attitudes are determined predominantly by internal considerations, because the internal politics of major nations are more apt to change significantly with the political leadership; and if such changes were to occur, what now appear to be harsh and recalcitrant positions taken by these would-be major powers on questions of concern to the major powers—particularly questions of arms control and political settlement in contiguous third world areas—might change substantially.

It must also be recognized that the opposition to limited arms control measures which is manifest by China and France can be explained in large part by the fact that both are at what might be termed a "take-off" stage in the development of national nuclear establishments. Neither would be prepared to quit at such a stage for nuclear disarmament, nor can either yet know what importance conventional military forces, which some propose to control, will come to have to them. Long-standing nuclear powers can and do tell the new nuclear nations that they will find nuclear weapons neither in themselves of great international value (a lesson Britain has apparently learned) nor a real substitute for conventional arms, particularly if these nations envisage themselves as major actors in international politics. But these are lessons apparently only to be learned by costly and perhaps dangerous direct experience.

An additional important internal determinant of the shape and texture of international politics to come is the will to align, assist, and contend, particularly in the continuing and burgeoning instances of instability and civil war potential. As has been suggested, the major threats to international order increasingly reside not in major confrontations but in minor instabilities and their consequent involvement of major powers.

These problems are international and are political as well as military; they serve to emphasize the basic question of national attitude toward "internationalism." Nations, as they mature, seem to become increasingly "other-directed"[3]—affected by and concerned with the attitudes and desires of other nations. This attitude is usually observed in international legal and economic activities before it is manifest in politics. It is also apparent in the tendency toward convergence among states with different social and economic and political systems. But it is particularly apparent in the appreciation of the place of rules and restraints in international intercourse. Adlai Stevenson observed in early 1964 that,

. . . the central trend of our times is the emergency of what, for lack of a better label, might be called a policy of cease-fire and peaceful change. . . . We may be approaching something close to a world consensus on such a policy. No analogy is ever perfect, but if the policy of containment stands for 'limited war,' then the policy of cease-fire perhaps stands for 'limited peace.' I believe this mutation is occurring simply because the H-bomb has made even 'limited war' too dangerous. Cease-fire and peaceful change may strike some as a curious way to describe a period so jammed by violence, by disorder, by quarrels among the nations—an era so lacking in law and order. But I do not speak wishfully; I speak from the record. It is precisely the fact that so much violence and so many quarrels *have not led to war* that puts a special mark on our times.[4]

Stevenson may have been wrong in sensing that there is an increasing tendency for nations to be interested in such restraints in peacetime as well as in wartime (about which there can be no question). But if he was correct, this development will cause an increase in international community that, matched or accompanied by a gradual and limited development of institutions created by limited arms control and other political agreements among the superpowers and perhaps increasingly among lesser states as well, could bring about a substantial increase in those aspects of international politics regulated not just by tacitly negotiated and reciprocally observed restraints but also by institutionalized patterns of resolution. Whether such developments could be fos-

[3]In the sense, used by David Riesman in *The Lonely Crowd* (New Haven, Conn.: Yale University Press, 1950), that their behavior is highly influenced by the standards of others rather than by tradition, training, or autonomous determination.

[4]Adlai Stevenson, "From Containment to Cease-Fire and Peaceful Change," in A. W. Cordier and W. Foote (eds.), *The Quest for Peace: The Dag Hammarskjold Memorial Lectures* (New York: Columbia University Press, 1965), pp. 51–66.

tered by progress in arms control and in their turn permit and encourage further progress in disarmament cannot be satisfactorily determined at this point, but will be considered in the next chapter.

These projected international political developments will be manifest to a nation as external determinants that can be classified as unit position, power, and system conditions. Unit position is a product of geography and allegiance. It was contended earlier that nations will become increasingly interested in arms control if allies become less attainable or more costly. There seems little doubt that allies are becoming harder to get and keep, both because of the power-political considerations described above and because of the developing strength and nationalism of middle and lesser powers. Major powers under these conditions can attempt to compensate for this increasing difficulty either by armament or by arms control.

The choice between armament and arms control will probably be partially determined by another alliance consideration: the interest of allies in the attainment of arms control among the superpowers. European allies on each side of Europe have increasingly pressed for *détente* and even entente among the superpowers. With the mellowing of the Federal Republic of Germany, Communist China seems the last major aligned power to oppose such trends. However, this does not necessarily suggest that these peace-loving powers will favor—or join— arms control measures. While still in the position of "catching up," not only China, but also France, has been and will continue to be hostile to significant arms control measures. On the other hand, the foremost "has-been" power, Britain, will continue to be interested in arms control measures that might save money and position. The central European powers, particularly West Germany, would probably oppose major arms control in Europe in favor of traditional reliance upon self- and Allied-help for security.

The cases of the weakling nations, whether aligned or not, will prove increasingly interesting. In the postwar years, these nations have sought arms from the major powers, thereby fomenting local arms races, such as those between India and Pakistan, those in the Middle East, and now those in Africa. But these arms races have invited greater major power intervention and influence not only in the affairs of the weakling nations, but increasingly in international affairs generally. Local arms races have also contributed to area instabilities, inviting foreign invasion, and the weaponry compounded has encouraged military coups and regimes in many such countries. Gradual recognition of these consequences, coupled with increasing resource pressure as it becomes clearer that economic development will be much more difficult than was believed in the early years of the "development decade," will undoubtedly increase the interest of weakling nations in arms control measures that might increase local and regional military stability, decrease the threat of the military to civilian regimes, and increase the possibility of commitment of most resources to economic development.

Thus, on balance, it might be concluded that unit position considerations would be apt to increase the interest of most powers in arms control measures and, hence, that assessment of external determinations by a given nation would increase its hopes that significant arms control measures might be attainable.

But these conclusions must be qualified somewhat by examination of power considerations. It was concluded earlier that conservative nations are apt to be enticed by those arms control measures that would tend to impede change, while more revolutionary nations would tend to oppose such measures. This conservatism seems to be increasing in the major nations of the world, excepting Communist China, and it may even increase in China with the advent of modernity and the exit of the Mao regime. The significance of conservatism for the prospects for arms control is trifold: First, measures promising to impede upsetting change (such as measures to curb arms races or nuclear proliferation) will gain increasing support; second, because of the major technological and economic differential between the superpowers and others, conservative nations will be able to indulge their conservative interest considerably before being significantly threatened by lesser powers; and third, even the revolutionary nations may seek arms control measures if it is believed or hoped that such measures will weaken the establishments of the more conservative states. This third possibility raises again the importance of the contention that the essential condition for arms control agreement is not coincidence of interest, but coincidence of instrument, which makes arms control in a world containing conservative and revolutionary states both more likely and more dangerous, for it may be grounded in varying assessments of its consequences for international position and change. For this reason, nations are apt to become increasingly wary of arms control measures as these become increasingly appealing.

The third and final external political category is the system, and its determinants are classed here as structure, environment, and process. To repeat an earlier contention, the system's structure is one of degenerating bipolarity. It has been argued that strong alliances tend to

encourage arms control measures among major powers and their diffusion to minor powers through major power leadership. It has also been
indicated that weak alliances could make arms control more acceptable
to the major powers because they could more easily alter alliances or
increase allies to compensate for risks incurred in arms control. These
propositions are not so contradictory as they may at first appear, for
each is particularly applicable to certain kinds of arms control measures, as will be shown in Chapter 9. At this point, it is important to
note that the weakening of the major postwar alliances can best be
described in terms of increasing political multipolarity, permitted by if
not wholly caused by continued military bipolarity. Thus, arms control
measures are possible among the superpowers. The key question, perhaps, over time will be the likely alignment of the "third world," either
in the continuing superpower confrontation or, perhaps, in the event of
increasing Communist Chinese militance and perhaps French trucu-
lence as supplements to the superpowers against the would-be superpowers. However, the latter possibility is neither likely nor necessary as
long as significant technological and economic differences separate
these two ranks.

The environmental system considerations are largely those of
economy and technology, since geography cannot be expected to
change significantly. Here, it has been argued, there seems little likelihood that the superpowers can break each other, but there is considerable possibility that they can break the would-be great powers unless
those powers are able to unite politically and economically to share the
knowledge and the costs of major nuclear and conventional military
activities that will be required of any great power. Such unity, however,
seems unlikely and this suggests that the challenges of these would-be
great powers will eventually subside and with them the hostility to arms
control.

There is one possible counter to this development: an apparent
residence of the superpowers upon a technological plateau. This may
encourage continued efforts to attain that plateau by the ambitious,
grounded on the mistaken belief that technological constancy is not
increasingly costly. On a plateau where qualitative jumps are not
possible, qualitative arms control becomes more possible while quantitative arms control, designed to curtail racing, becomes more significant. The key factor here will be the perception of this plateau and
estimates of its temporal extent by the superpowers, who might then
engage in bilateral control, and by the lesser powers, who might then
either seek to attain it, thereby disinteresting themselves (and perhaps

the challenged superpowers) in arms control or to settle for lower and less costly postures. Assessment of these conditions by any power considering its attitude toward arm control will be both difficult and unclear in its implications.

The final major determinant of national interest in arms control is difficult to predict. The intellectual condition of national interest is the availability of promising measures to achieve the arms control objectives which interest nations. National efforts at analysis and proposition of arms control problems and measures will probably increase as other conditions encourage increased national interest in arms control. It is to be expected, therefore, that the creation of new and improved arms control measures will increase and, thus, that national interest and action will become more attractive and possible. Whether there will also occur innovation, within the nation and particularly its bureaucracy, that will enable these measures to gain approval and become policy is a subject for administrative political analysis rather than international political analysis and cannot be undertaken in this analysis. Whether bureaucratic national innovation will produce arms control efforts culminating in innovation in the international system will depend heavily upon the success of presently operant measures, such as the Antarctica treaty, the hotline, and the nuclear testban treaty. However, the predictable prospects for further multinational arms control measures are the subject of the concluding chapter.

CHAPTER 9

The Prospects
for Arms Control

The preceding analysis of the determinants of national interest in arms control suggests that there will develop general and increasing interest in arms control in the coming decade. Potential determinants for arms control cannot be easily cumulated, not only because attitudes toward specific measures cannot be measured, but also because this must be a predictive analysis. But even if tentative conclusions about the interest resulting from individual determinants could be cumulated, that cumulation would probably be misleading unless a synergistic factor were added. Synergy, that feature of combination by which the unity can be greater than the sum of its parts, is particularly applicable to international politics because of the impact of considerations of atmosphere, spirit, entente, and other immaterials upon policy and interaction. That is, the cumulation of considerations may tend to be exponential, particularly in the effect of agreement upon the possibility of further agreement and in the impact of instances of worsened political relations upon other aspects of relation. Such phenomena, understandable and widely recognized when translated into morale, trust, and suspicion, must probably be multiplied in magnitude, and their impact cannot even be guessed without analyzing the specific situation and measures under consideration or implementation.

These admitted limitations upon the accuracy of specific forecasts do not vitiate the worth of the present study, for that worth lies mainly in the comprehensive demonstration of a method of analysis and in the general conclusions that can be reached. Each of these can then be specifically applied and pursued in further study and action.

The preconditions of arms control have been examined at length, both the determinants of national attitudes and interest in arms control and the possible approaches to arms control arrangements. Chapter 8 projected the national policy preconditions. The key questions remaining to be answered are: Given the condition requirements outlined and the national attitudes projected, will national plans and actions coincide to bring about international arms control outcomes? What arms control measures seem possible or even likely? How can such measures be attained, implemented, and maintained in the terms of the analysis of the requisites and possibilities for this as presented abstractly in Part II?

There is a striking divergence of views about the international conditions most favoring agreement on arms control measures. It is sometimes argued that arms control agreement depends upon either a condition of international balance or, apparently contrarily, upon a situation of international crisis. It is sometimes argued that political settlement is a precondition for arms control, while at other times it is argued that arms control must precede political settlement.

Two different contentions should be distinguished in the argument that political settlement must precede arms control. One is that without political settlement there will be no arms control because nations will be unwilling to accept or agree to any substantial measures. This might be because they would not wish to deprive themselves of the tools or capacity to take action in a dispute or it might be because of a national distrust of uncertainty (about a situation of controlled armaments) and preference for "certain" tension and danger, perhaps of a more limited scale than might be risked in a world of controlled arms. Those who argue that arms control cannot precede political settlement do not necessarily argue that arms control will follow settlement. Advocates of arms control as a necessary and logical consequence of political settlement reason that once conflict is settled arms or some arms are no longer needed. This will be true if weapons were designed with specific and unique capabilities tailored to the previous conflict situation. And it may be true if, in some fashion, the elimination of points of conflict is not followed by the development or discovery of other conflict. In either case, the obsolescence of arms would presumably encourage unilateral disarmament rather than negotiated disarmament, although negotiated disarmament might be sought for whatever nonsubstantive benefits it might offer, such as increased intercourse and experience of agreement.

The second possible reason why political settlement might be thought a prerequisite of arms control is the argument that, without settlement, arms control—even if attained—cannot work, because the international order will uncover other conflicts encouraging rearmament, war, or other consequences that the undertaken arms control was intended to avert.

However, both of these arguments, realistic although they appear, fail to cope with the fundamental question: Can arms control be undertaken in a situation of continuing political conflicts? If this is possible, it will be so either because some armaments are themselves superfluous or because arms control can in some way *replace* some part of the defense establishment as a military or political instrument of national policy. It could do this by performing the tasks of the eliminated arms or the constrained military or by rendering the performance of those tasks unnecessary.

The basic tasks of arms are four: deterrence, defense, offense, and retaliation. The *deterrent* task would be performed, at least in part, by agreements constraining "offensive" capability or decision through the provision of sanctions or by agreements deterring armament or rearmament by threat of arms racing which would eliminate the possibility of unilateral benefit. The *defense* task would be performed by an arms control measure constraining the capability of an attacker to achieve surprise. It is less likely that arms control measures could perform the *offensive* tasks of arms, mostly because of the essential limiting nature of arms control. But agreements to forego or curtail developments such as antiballistic missile or civil defense capabilities might serve the offensive interests of the military. In any event, in this nuclear age nations might consider the general failure of arms control systems to replace or augment offensive capabilities unimportant or even desirable. The final, *retaliatory* task might be performed by an agreement that provided satisfactory sanctions to replace traditional measures of "self-help." It does appear possible, then, that some arms control measures would perform part of the military establishment's tasks of deterrence, defense, offense, and retaliation. Thus, arguments that political settlement must precede arms control measures need not always hold.

The presence of political conflict has encouraged the development and maintenance of military capability, and the combined presence of political conflict and military capability has undoubtedly contributed to international tensions. Advocates of arms control often argue that measures of arms control might indeed encourage political settlement by lessening international tensions. It might be expected that the tensions removed or decreased by arms control measures would be predominantly those arising from the nature or usage of weapons, rather

than from the presence of international conflict. But achievement of
limited specific agreement may also change national assessments of
adversary intentions as well as capabilities, and may thereby reduce
tensions not arising directly from weaponry. This appears to have been
one effect of agreement upon the limited nuclear testban treaty, for
example.

There are several other ways in which arms control might encourage political settlement. First, a working system of arms controls designed to cope with dangerous and provocative international situations
might be considered evidence that ways could be found to resolve other
problems. Second, arms control measures that were considered significant limitations upon the use of the military establishment might
provide an incentive to settle disputes politically by the fact that they
could not be won or even sought so easily militarily. Indeed, this is
precisely what is feared by many military opponents of arms control.
And it is something to fear should military incapacity be tantamount
necessarily to over-all political weakness—but only if the arms control
measures did not in themselves contribute positively to the attainment
of national desires such as security.

Basically, arguments over precedence between political settlement
and arms control can be broken down into questions of which comes
first—military establishments or political differences. If the development of a military establishment can be attributed to the existence of
political quarrels, as indeed it basically can, then one might argue it is
foolish to seek to deal with symptomatic armaments rather than causal
conflicts. But this neglects the role of interaction in multiplying arms
which often in effect cancel each other out. And it does not recognize
an important fact: That conflict precedes arms does suggest that while
there is conflict arms will be maintained; but which arms, how many
arms, and how they will be employed is not indicated by such genetic
argument. And that conflict precedes arms does not necessarily indicate
that the way to reduce arms is to remove conflict, for the arms themselves may create or foster tensions, which make political settlement
particularly difficult. As David Singer has written,

. . . while accepting the proposition that unresolved conflicts and their ac-
companying tensions will certainly lead nations into armament programs, the
arms-first position also recognizes that between competing nations which are
heavily armed, there *must* be an impressive level of tension. Moreover—and
this is the crucial point—once the armament process has gotten under way,
tensions cannot be materially reduced and political conflicts cannot be resolved; the weapons have added a new variable to the equation, and until

they are removed, the equation remains insoluble. The point to be emphasized is that just because political conflicts and tensions normally *appear*
prior to armaments, it does not at all follow that they can therefore be made
to *disappear* prior to the armaments.[1]

Thus, in a sense the important question about political settlement
and arms control is not which precedes or even which is more fundamental, but rather whether nations can have one before or without the
other. The achievement of limited arms control measures in recent
years has altered the emphasis of this question to large-scale arms
control and disarmament.

There is considerable dispute about the time or context in which
such substantial arms control or disarmament agreements might be
attainable. In most national proposals for substantial disarmament,
there has been implicit the principle that the first phase of general
disarmament might be a designed improvement in the military balance.
And it is true that most of the limited arms control measures undertak-
en, such as the unilateral increase in missile invulnerability, the hotline,
and the limited nuclear testban treaty, have contributed to military
balance broadly conceived. But it is often argued that nations can or
will only undertake such measures if there is a considerable degree of
balance in their relative military postures at the outset, so that the
measures improve rather than create balance. Such considerations can
explain de Gaulle's adamant abstention from disarmament negotiations
and the attitude of Communist China, which is believed comparable.
Just as in general nations may not insist on negotiating from strength
but are very hesitant to negotiate from weakness, so nations appear
generally unwilling to undertake arms control negotiations, to say nothing of agreements, from positions of military inferiority.

But if nations appear generally unwilling to negotiate on arms
control except from positions of relative military balance, this does not
at all imply that nations in such position will indeed negotiate or agree.
The apparently contradictory argument of some that nations will undertake disarmament only in a crisis[2] is an argument that nations are

---

[1] J. David Singer, *Deterrence, Arms Control, and Disarmament* (Columbus,
Ohio: Ohio State University Press for the Mershon Center for Education in National Security, 1962), pp. 179–180.

[2] This argument has been made by Herman Kahn and by Thomas Schelling.
See Anthony J. Wiener and Herman Kahn (eds.), *Crises and Arms Control*,
HI–180–RR. (Harmon-on-Hudson, New York: Hudson Institute, 1962), especially
chap. 7; see also Thomas Schelling's discussion of "crash" arms control in "Reciprocal Measures for Arms Stabilization," in Brennan (ed.), *Arms Control, Disarma-*

highly unlikely to accept disarmament under any circumstances except those in which the international order is collapsing and the entire international system is thereupon transformed. Such "crash" disarmament is made even less likely by the obvious mutual interest in averting the collapse that could "necessitate" such drastic change.

Similarly, in terms of systemic conditions, it seems likely that arms control arrangements will be more easily reached in a relatively bipolar world where multiple interests are minimized. Yet, as has been suggested earlier, the multipolarization of international politics may tend to restore the traditional flexibility in which nations can rely upon external increments to their military strength and in which nations can therefore better afford arms control and even disarmament. It would appear also that optimism about the way of the world and particularly the evolution of the developing states would encourage agreements upon arms control because there would be neither great fear of an adverse alliance nor particular need for armaments in policing these new states. Yet, because disarmament and most current measures of arms control have been static and conservative, a pessimism about the development of the international contest for allegiance might well encourage greater efforts to stabilize relations through such arrangement.

The difficulty in selecting among each of these incompatible possibilities suggests that attention must be given to specific measures rather than to arms control of any general sort. But it also suggests a useful distinction between short-run and limited arms control measures, which are perhaps more likely to be achieved in conditions of *détente,* bipolarity, and optimism—as were the nuclear testban, the hotline, and defense budget cuts—and between long-run and more substantial arms control measures, which may be more likely to result from continued fear, multipolar tendencies in international politics, and less optimism about the emergence of a compatible world. That there have not yet been such substantial agreed measures in the postwar world reflects the absence or weakness of these conditions as well as the grave difficulties of achieving multinational agreements over important matters in an ominous period. It could be said, however, that the Washington Agreements of 1922 were of this type; and a general antiproliferation agreement or measures of substantial disarmament would also qualify.

---

ment, and National Security (New York: Braziller, 1961), pp. 183–184. Further, see John Strachey, *On the Prevention of War* (London: Macmillan, 1962), pp. 311–312.

The international order is apparently beginning to evolve from a period of *détente,* bipolarity, and optimism—which is best suited to short-run arms control agreements—toward a period characterized by developing disintegration of alliances and pessimism about the possibilities of political and economic development in the new state decisively favorable to either side, coupled with the continuing fear of military disaster multiplied somewhat by both the development of new nuclear establishments and the increase in relatively internal wars. These developments may present opportunities for longer-term arms control arrangements. But arrangements involving the developing states may well be preceded and accompanied by political-military agreements in Europe. And both will most likely be preceded by further limited arrangements arising from the persisting superpower confrontation. Thus, while the analyst or policy maker will probably look increasingly to Europe and then to the "third world" for opportunities for arms control, he can still more profitably look first to the superpowers.

There seems no chance of general and comprehensive disarmament—at least not in the era of the superpower confrontation—if only (but not only) because the superpowers could not make it general and so would not make it comprehensive. However, there may be opportunities for substantial disarmament conceived in terms of another organizing principle. The most immediate of such prospects is generally referred to as a "bomber bonfire" in which each side would destroy obsolete and obsolescent bombers in the other's presence. Such a measure would keep these planes out of the hands of the unstable new states to whom they would not be obsolete. The desirability of such a "bonfire" may have been somewhat lessened by the expansion of war in South Vietnam, where it was found that big jet bombers are inefficient in many operations, while small prop planes (many of which the United States had given or sold to other states) proved less obsolescent than previously thought. Nonetheless, early-generation jets, most of which remain mothballed, could feed such fires.

Another measure of substantial disarmament would be to lower the level of forces abroad or to alter the stationing of such forces. In Europe such changes would necessarily be parts of broader developments and are better discussed in that context. In the "third world," such curtailments seem less likely as wars of national liberation and civil insurrection seem more frequent, for the United States still is—as long as it envisages itself as such—the world's chief policeman; and until regional peace forces (like that constructed by the Organization of American States to replace command over American troops in Santo Domingo) or

United Nations peace-police forces (like that formed by the Scandinavians or like those organized *ad hoc* to serve in the Mideast, the Congo, and Cyprus) are formed and funded, the United States is likely to retain all the foreign-stationed troops it has. Still, the outlook for some sort of multinational, if not necessarily international, forces in the coming decade may not be so bleak as current difficulties in the United Nations suggest. The Soviets have a growing interest in slowing the destabilizing change in much of Asia and potentially Africa. It would take greater optimism than most analysts can muster to expect stability to increase in these areas in the next decade and greater confidence than their experience would justify for the Soviets to agree to take their chances with insurrection and "neo-imperialist" intervention. Hence, the possibility of regional peace-police forces may permit such arms control measures not just in Europe, where political evolution seems likely to bring that about, but in other areas of the world as well.

Also increasingly possible will be development and recognition of spheres of control, influence, interest, and concern, coupled perhaps with agreements of nonintervention in internal conflicts. The clear and understandable obsession of the United States with the Western hemisphere and of the Soviet Union with Eastern Europe provide the possible basis for increased recognition of such spheres. In addition, the status and economic cost of the Soviet adventure in Cuba and the painfulness of the American adventure in Vietnam seem likely to teach lessons to each side about its vital interests. And because the problem in such cases is how to get out (if one hasn't been able to stay out) before departure becomes too costly, arrangements recognizing such spheres may assist in getting and staying out.

Some Westerners will cry that this would consign millions to slavery and seal the eventual erosion of Western freedom, and some Communists will undoubtedly claim that such an understanding would thwart the forces of history. But the Communist world is irreconcilably split on issues short of life and death and the Western world, in its more traditionally civilized way, is already showing the signs of division of interest and independence of activity. Consequently, neither superpower will be consigning territory to its adversary alone; and while each adversary will be eliminating its kin, it will not be eliminating its kith from the international struggle. Thus, the United States will probably have to relinquish its active interests in Eastern Europe to Western Europe and its interests in Southern Asia to the Soviet Union and China (and perhaps to an Indian-Japanese axis). No region will lack the competition that Western liberal ideology claims will bring it closer to freedom, and no region will lack the possibility of relating its fate to that of its immediate neighbors, as traditional Russian geopolitical thought has sought. In their purest political form, such spherical arrangements do not seem much like arms control. But they would most likely be accompanied by agreements limiting or eliminating military aid and tutelage and especially presence by the major powers, probably with further understandings that proliferation of nuclear weapons, delivery vehicles, and other technological wonders would be forbidden.

If the vision of the world underlying this analysis is basically correct, such political change is not a visionary possibility, but rather a developing actuality. Consequently, the important question is how will the superpowers capitalize upon this development to insure that these areas, as they gravitate toward their traditional roles as competitive neighbors of adversary states less dependent upon their previous postwar suzerains, do not take with them military establishments prone to local instabilities and threats to the security of their previous suzerains. The implications of this development for military aid, especially nuclear dispersion, and for joint programs, like the Multilateral Nuclear Force, are clear. Whether they will be recognized and accepted in time is not.

Although these long-term political developments are more interesting, more important to the superpower confrontation in the next several years will be lesser measures, such as extension of the nuclear testban to underground explosions, cut-offs of production of nuclear warheads and delivery vehicles, limitations on national programs of civil defense and ballistic missile defense, and reduction in defense spending. Unless the United States alone develops multiple-warhead missiles, the Soviet Union seems likely to continue to narrow the numerical gap between its nuclear forces and those of the United States. Should this trend continue, there will be no convincing intrinsic reasons why such agreements—which would be economical and would likely improve the tenor of relations among the two powers at a time when each faces increasing competition within its own alliance—could not be reached. Nonetheless, it is possible that the United States will continue to insist upon massively superior nuclear forces to preserve its potential counterforce threat to defend or press its interests in Europe and the "third world." Such an unwillingness to accept approximate nuclear parity, while it need not preclude agreement upon these lesser measures, will probably render such stabilizing or equalizing measures less acceptable and less attainable and hence shift interest to other measures not directly affecting superpower forces and capabilities. But even if both sides are willing to accept something approximating nuclear parity, incentives to reach agreement on such measures as those under consideration here will probably reside more in nonsecurity considerations than in such security considerations as the risk of war and the magnitude of its destructiveness should it come. Both sides' capabilities are so massive and so easily multiplied that curtailment of the magnitude of destruction would require massive disarmament, and curtailment of the risk of war would require other arrangements.

Such other arrangements, like improvements in command, control, and communications brought about by joint read-out of radar and other early warning systems, and further provisions against war by accident, inadvertence, mischief, or miscalculation, seem quite possible. Also, arrangements such as communications links might well be extended to other notable nuclear nations, such as Great Britain, France, and eventually Communist China, in an effort to guard against the rising danger of mischief and catalysis. These are not major measures nor will they compromise the security and effectiveness of any power not contemplating aggressive or militant action. Consequently, there is no particular reason why they should not be implemented whenever the powers concerned conclude that they are both desirable and domestically acceptable, for their technical aspects should prove manageable.

But perhaps the area of major immediate concern is the development and strengthening of restraints and constraints typified by the tacit agreement against nuclear proliferation and the United Nations pronouncement against orbiting nuclear weapons. It is widely suspected that there is, in effect, an agreement among the nuclear nations not to be the first to use nuclear weapons. NATO strategy in Europe, particularly over Berlin, has required periodical statement of a threat of such first use; and while Western conventional strength in Europe has improved somewhat and Eastern strength estimates have been revised downward, political settlement in Europe would seem the only way of making such an agreement against first use of nuclear weapons acceptable to the United States and Western Europe.

Perhaps equally significant are possible tacit agreements on city avoidance in nuclear war and other restraints, such as on destruction of civilian targets in conventional war and on the use of chemical-bacteriological-radiological (CBR) weapons in any war. The Soviets have scorned city avoidance as impracticable, and Western planners have recognized that the Soviets have not yet developed the nuclear strength in numbers and perhaps accuracy to be able effectively and confidently to agree to city avoidance. Yet there is a lingering suspicion in many minds that in a nuclear war the Soviets would seek to avoid destroying cities, at least as long as the Western powers did the same.

There are other restraints, however, that have more immediate concern, particularly those against the use and even deployment of CBR weapons. The danger arises from the fact that some of these weapons (such as those similar to tear gas) are indeed more humane than most weapons and may well be effective. Thus, the advanced nations whose research has developed these sophisticated and expensive weapons will be tempted to employ them in their "policing" operations and in "national liberation" wars in which they have become embroiled. The developing states are still underdeveloped in chemical warfare, and if the psychological barrier has not been broken already by American use of some such weapons in Vietnam, it might well be broken by further use of such weapons by any nation. An adversary underdeveloped in sophisticated chemical warfare might respond to "humane" chemical weapons by the use of lethal chemicals and gases, such as mustard gas, and so end fifty years of cautious restraint.

This brief assessment of the superpower confrontation and arms control possibilities suggests that there will be considerable opportunities for agreement. Once the political bases for such agreement exist, it should be possible to render the proposed agreements more promising. This could be done by employing the analysis of administration, adjudication, information, and particularly control, accession, mediation, elaboration, specification, and alteration, in order to construct specific agreements based upon a clear understanding of the possible function of each of these elements and incorporating various devices and provisions suggested in Chapters 6 and 7.

In most cases, such superpower agreements would only formalize what appear to be tacit restraints and constraints presently accepted. The reason why there seems so little desirable or possible of achievement by formal agreement among the superpowers is twofold: First, the military relations between the nations can be described as an increasingly entrenched military stalemate; and second, most of the international political and military problems arise out of the engagement in Europe and the development of the new states. It is to these areas that analysts must turn, and it is in these areas that further arms control arrangements must be sought.

Most substantial arms control provisions for Europe involve some degree of "disengagement"—from neutralization coupled with political settlement, which would include reunification of Germany, through demilitarization of some zone in Central Europe, to denuclearization of the defense of Berlin or East and West Germany. Discussion of disengagement in Europe generally centers upon the strength and justification of fears of German resurgence plus the prospect and fears of a vacuum in Central Europe. It should prove more useful to ask, not whether disengagement in Europe is possible or likely, but what the various possible courses of political development in Central Europe are, how likely each seems, and what role arms control measures might play in the attainment or obstruction of each. This study cannot undertake such a complex political study, but the relations between the German question and arms control in Europe must be remembered when assessing the prospects for arms control.

If the full Gaullist image of a strong and independent Europe materializes, West Germany will be subservient to France; Eastern Europe and perhaps even Russia will be drawn toward the West in a re-establishment of the traditional European balancing game. Because it is unlikely that a reunited Germany would remain answerable to the French, and because it is even more unlikely that the Soviet Union would permit such reunification were it to be Western-oriented, there seems little reason to expect German reunification. Indeed, if de Gaulle should not live another five to ten years, it is difficult to see his successor enticing Eastern Europe into the Western game. If, as seems likely, the French nation is basically Gaullist in its desire to resume a responsible political role in Europe and elsewhere and if France is prepared to pay the nuclear economic price for that role, it also seems likely that no one beyond de Gaulle could manage to draw the East into a predominantly Western European balancing game. A France without de Gaulle would probably gradually become subject to political (and perhaps eventually military) leadership by West Germany. This development would be the more likely should the American Multilateral Nuclear Force be established, for that would drive the French further from America and at the same time strengthen the eventual German claim to political and military responsibility. In that event, while France might eventually submit to West German political leadership, the possibility that the Soviet Union would itself re-enter Europe or even allow East Germany further independence seems minimal.

The other root possibility is an approximate continuation of present arrangements, in which the superpowers exercise a condominium of sorts over Germany and, to decreasing extents, over their remaining spheres in Europe and periodically threaten to express their confrontation on European soil. Such an arrangement seems doomed to eventual deterioration, and the pain of that degeneration may be directly proportional to the length of the stay of old allies. There can be no question that both Eastern and Western Europe would prefer to have the superpowers out—so long as there is no significant threat from Germany. It is increasingly clear also that police commitments elsewhere and cold-war weariness will take an increasing toll on American desire or willingness to stay, particularly when coupled with the "ingratitude" of the Europeans for all that the American presence has done since the war. Nonetheless, the end of the American and Soviet presence in Germany is not now in sight.

Although some disagree and many are disquieted, there seems little opportunity for political settlement in Europe in the near future. It may come to pass that a strong Western Europe can bring about the pacification of Central Europe over the next decade. But in the meantime—and particularly until the strength and direction of the Gaullist tendencies in Europe are better known—the place of arms control in Europe will likely be occupied by limited measures designed to stabilize the balance and make the military postures safer. There are such opportunities for increasing the military liaison inspection forces that were provided for in the Potsdam Agreements and which are allowed to wander around both halves of Germany. There are further possibilities for establishment of observation posts and inspection teams at key transport facilities to insure against mobilization for conventional attack. Indeed, these measures, which might eventually be instituted elsewhere in the inspection and control of substantial disarmament agreements, could receive interesting trials in this peculiar "hothouse" confrontation called the "Two Germanies." However, such arrangements might meet with hostility from a France convinced of the incredibility of an Eastern attack upon a nuclearly armed West and at the same time anxious to return Germany to Europe from the hands of the wartime allies.

In summary, it might be said with only slight exaggeration that arms control and Gaullism in Europe are alternatives tending to be mutually exclusive or unacceptable. It is hardly surprising that France has refused to participate in recent disarmament talks, not only because as a "catcher-up" she is disinclined to consider abandoning her quest for status as a major military power, but also because her conception of Europe leaves little room for arms control arrangements, particularly when those arrangements would be exercised largely by the superpowers. However, French hostility to arms control need not be detrimental to the basic interests arms control is sought to serve. The objectives of Gaullists—namely, disengagement of the superpowers from Central

Europe and restoration of more traditional patterns of politics in greater Europe—are not necessarily inconsistent with those to be served by arms control. What will happen, however, is that if Gaullism succeeds and if France (with possible assistance from a nuclear Great Britain and a wealthy West Germany) develops into a significant nuclear nation, it will be realized that in this nuclear age politics cannot be played with such abandon as they once were in Europe, for they are immensely more expensive and dreadfully more dangerous. Thus, when the costs of maintaining substantial nuclear capability are coupled with the dangers bound to arise out of the confrontation of a nuclear Europe with other nuclear powers, Europe will become interested in the kinds of arms control measures that are designed to make nuclear weapons acceptable "sidekicks" and usable (declaratorily if not explosively) sidearms. Thus, arrangements improving command, control, and communications provisions encouraging mutual restraint in expensive development, and provisions insuring the relative uniqueness of the possession will come into favor. These developments are easily anticipated by the major powers on the basis of their own experience, but apparently cannot be conveyed from a great power to a would-be great power. The omnipresent brooding will be over whether conditions will force such realization soon enough.

A compelling reason to doubt that such realization of the limits and dangers of nuclear weapons will come soon enough is the fact that the distance that separated the three significant nuclear powers from emergent France and China was much greater than any subsequent separation of this pair from nations like West Germany, India, Israel, Egypt, and perhaps others, can be. The simple multiplication of nuclear powers increases dangers in and likelihoods of and even incentives for use of such weapons. And when that multiplication takes place among nations that have neither the technological capability nor the financial possibility of developing controls and observing restraints that the major powers do, the dangers and hence the challenge to arms control are immense.

The possibility of nuclear proliferation among the developing states might be met in various ways. An agreement among the nuclear powers to not assist in any way the development of nuclear weapons and delivery systems, coupled with a pledge by those nations not to undertake such development or receive such assistance, would seem the most promising. But additional, stricter controls over the "peaceful" uses of nuclear materials and energy might obstruct the effort, and establishment by agreement of nuclear-free zones might lessen the incentive. All these measures seem possible, although their universality might be limited by hysterical objections from such nations as Indonesia and by understandable neighborly fears of such nations as India. It would appear, however, that the world needs all the nonproliferation agreements it can get.

It would be dangerous, though, to believe that nuclear proliferation is the sole or even major problem concerning the developing nations with which arms control measures might cope. Local arms races and their explosion by military assistance from outside become a major sporadic problem that arms control might help to resolve. In such cases, control would probably take the form of joint agreements by the major powers to restrict their assistance and by local states to accept limits. Indeed, such situations might prove to be very useful laboratories for the development of inspection and verification capabilities and even control techniques and systems that might later be applied to great-power limitation. It is unfortunate that developing nations tend to be so protective about their new-found and perhaps short-lived sovereignty and so would probably oppose such arrangements. But it is also promising that these nations are small and weak enough that, should a situation arise where multinational intervention, perhaps under the United Nations, were required, such international activity might be possible. The possibility is at least worth bearing in mind as instabilities multiply and spread in the coming years.

In the meantime, the development of restraints in local, predominantly guerrilla, warfare merits much attention. The potential problem with chemical weapons has already been considered. Further restraints likely to prove desirable would involve civilians, prisoners, and sanctuaries. It is unfortunate that big-power involvement in such conflicts as that in Vietnam tends to undermine rather than to strengthen such patterns of political and military action. If there is an area worthy of considerable thought and experimentation, it is this conjunction of arms control, limited war, and counterinsurgency. So little is known about what goes on, let alone how it might be curtailed or otherwise altered, that the arms control analyst has little to say, even though guerrilla warfare is in many ways the most restrained and constrained of all types of warfare.

It is also possible that newly developing states will be able to serve constructively in the implementation of arms control arrangements through provision of good offices, of channels of communication (as between Communist China and the United States), and of contingents for United Nations or other international police, peace, or inspection forces. Such activities may contribute to the development of responsibility by these nations, which would in itself be a major contribution to the objectives sought through arms control measures: reducing the risk of war and its destructiveness should it occur.

Any examination of the prospects for arms control in the superpower confrontation, in the European engagement, and in the developing states is bound to be unsatisfying by the very uncertain nature of both international politics and the ordering devices and arrangements termed arms control. The significant determination of these two concluding chapters is that there appear to be multiple opportunities for the employment of arms control. The question, then, is whether there exist plans, programs, and concepts of arms control adaptable to these circumstances that can promise some likelihood of success. This question emphasizes the importance of the application of creative thought by analysts and policy makers, not just to specific problems, but also to the concept of arms control and its possible expression in instruments taking full advantage of the opportunities for implementation and maintenance as examined in some detail in Chapters 6 and 7.

Ways might be found to overcome the difficulties in inducing accession by applying the principle of staging to procedural aspects of ratification and accession as well as to substantive provisions. Furthermore, provisions might be included for reservation and partial deratification in the event that a nation felt unable to comply with some provisions but still desired to participate in the rest of an agreement and such alteration were acceptable to others.

It has been suggested that any arms control agreement will be subject to both internal strain and external stress. Internal strain will arise from the apparent natural tendency of nations to seek to bend an agreement to better serve their particular interests. External stress will arise from changes in the environs or interests of the parties and from malfunctions of the agreement. Internal strain will be coped with by implementation provisions for administration, adjudication, information, control, and extension and termination. Possible development and formulation of such provisions were discussed extensively in Chapter 7. External stress will be coped with by maintenance provisions for subsequent accession, resolution, elaboration and specification, and alteration. These possible provisions were developed in Chapter 6. It should be remembered, however, that the continual presence of change within and challenge to such an agreement may not be entirely ominous, for imbalance allowing for and encouraging creativeness, leadership, and achievement could prove necessary and meritorious.

Conclusion

Predicting the future is not in itself a difficult task—nor is it necessarily a responsible activity. But predicting the future conscientiously or predicting the future when policy is to be based upon those predictions is still apt to be debilitatingly difficult. This burden may be lightened if the predictions are explicitly stated and if they are expressed in testable forms so that error can be easily detected and considered in any continued reliance upon the predictions and so that prediction itself can be improved.

Are these predictions in Part III, then, testable? They were not put in absolute form, but they are expressible as propositions that can be confirmed or disconfirmed over time. Not only their validity but also their relevance is subject to the considerable limitation that it is not yet known what factors do indeed determine foreign policy and national interaction. Thus, any prediction, as has been continually indicated, must make considerable assumptions about causal relations. Under these circumstances, is there reason for testing these predictions?

Admittedly, the predictions presented in this study are not satisfactorily "scientific." Prediction is an intellectual endeavor that is not yet fully developed methodologically; and the data are not well enough collected and assayed and ensconced in promising or confirmed theoretical constructions to enable these predictions to be declared infallible. But if arms control is to offer a promise to interested nations and to raise interest resulting in national quests, then the task of improving the art and validity of prediction is well undertaken. And, thus, it should be worthwhile to increasingly test these predictions as the present decade progresses. But for now it will probably prove more worthwhile to devote most analysis, imagination, and creation to international politics in general and to arms control in particular.

Such analysis and theoretical construction in foreign policy and national interaction should contribute to our knowledge of—and hence eventually our ability to predict—the determinants of politics and hence of arms control. Such analysis and creation in arms control studies can contribute to the development not only of theories of when and why arms control will be sought nor only of in what ways arms control may be attained, implemented, and maintained, but also of policy-oriented "engineering" propositions about the ways in which arms control sought may more effectively be gained and more satisfactorily be maintained.

In general, it might be argued that the sole policy function of the scholar is to delineate underlying necessities and to assess possible consequences. Louis Halle, a policy maker turned academician, has written that the scholar

. . . should not, therefore, think himself capable of saying how the practical problems of the daily chaos should be solved, of telling the practitioner what to do. . . . "It is the gift of civilized man," Walter Lippmann once wrote, ". . . that he can at times see through the transient and the complicated to the simple and the certain, and that he can live by that vision, and with it master or endure his lot." The exercise of this gift is the scholar's real business. It is his real business (again in Lippmann's words) to see "the necessary amidst confusion and insignificance, and by the light which it furnishes to see more clearly how to act with purpose." The scholar's business is direction.[3]

Such advice and prescription is generally sensible, but its application to arms control might be modified slightly. The policy maker is quite aware of the reality underlying armament and undermining disarmament. But he may not be sufficiently aware of the developing reality that underlies the processes of arms control and might be employed in the construction of arms control measures serving national and multinational objectives. The general lesson of the difficulty of controlling arms has been quickly learned, if it was not already known, by statesmen and policy makers of the postwar period. This period has taught that where the focus had been previously on reducing arms, now the focus must be on reducing aims: reducing the aims of policy to avoid war by political conflict and design and reducing the aims of arms control to achieve measures to reduce the danger and destructiveness of war.

There are various strategies which have been and might be employed in the face of the difficulty of controlling arms. One is to work harder with the traditional tools. This has generally been the approach of advocates both within as well as without government. Another is to adapt to the difficulties. Adaptation may involve cutting the problem down to the size of the available techniques (institutions, tools, and conceptions). This often unrealistic approach has an important, increasingly popular, and often quite realistic variant: doing what can be done now and hoping that more will be possible later. Thus, one analyst,

[3]Louis J. Halle, "On Teaching International Relations," *Virginia Quarterly Review*, 40 (1964), pp. 24–25.

after a study of the problems of inspection, concluded that because

. . . far-reaching disarmament measures inescapably imply far-reaching inspection and control arrangements . . . , if the end of the disarmament road
is to be reached, there must be revolutionary prerequisite changes—changes
that substitute the will to cooperate for today's pattern of international conflict and produce in the Communist world and elsewhere the conditions
that make full inspection either acceptable or no longer necessary. No one can
predict that such revolutionary changes will take place. The disarmament
problem is thus to identify and undertake those initial measures that will
start the world on the disarmament path, provide adequate grounds for confidence on the part of suspicious governments, and to avoid confrontation of
those ultimate issues that cannot be solved under today's conditions. In this
way the passage of time and the developing experience of arms limitations
might lead to the necessary transformations.[4]

This attitude has been implicit in the postwar achievement of such
arms control measures as the limited nuclear testban treaty and the
hotline. But its optimistic assumption of the reconstructive impact of
such measures upon the international order makes it less than a reliable
exclusive approach to resolution of problems present and future problems.

Thus, there is also a role for a third fundamental strategy: innovation that will develop techniques the size of the problem. At the easiest
level, it is always recognized that technological innovation permits
novel weapons development, but it is not always recognized that technological innovation is not the only innovation relevant to international
affairs. There may be innovation in international politics that will bring
about greater possibilities for arms control. In a sense, achievement of
détente can be viewed as such innovation, or at least as reintroduction
of a previous innovation, just as Gaullism might be viewed as an
innovation tending to limit the prospects of arms control. Such political
innovation is not easily classified or anticipated. It would almost certainly be difficult to engineer such innovation as a part of a national
strategy to cope with the continuing difficulty in attaining arms control.
But the arms control implications of political innovation will be worthy
of national attention.

A third type is innovation of international forms that might be
used to construct arms control measures. A recent study by the Arms

[4]Lawrence S. Finkelstein, "Arms Inspection," published as *International Conciliation*, no. 540, November (1962), p. 13.

Control and Disarmament Agency concluded in part that

> . . . treaties are not essentially enforceable, and thus . . . the customary treaty instruments may not be suitable vehicles for the arms control route to world order. It is beyond the scope of this study to suggest what can be done to devise new treaty forms and concepts to replace the ones that have been relatively unsatisfactory in the past. Possibly . . . treaties between sovereign powers can never be sufficiently reliable for a nation to abandon, or even severely limit, its capabilities for protecting all of its vital interests. We see no reason, however, to becloud the future of arms control by tying it to existing, unsatisfactory forms of treaties. Possibly adequate machinery providing for peaceful change . . . may permit long strides toward world order through arms limitations. In addition, however, we believe that a thorough, uninhibited investigation should be made of the possibility of making radical improvements in the art of treaty-making. In a dynamic world, stability can be achieved only through constant experimentation and modification.[5]

It is such innovation in international forms, some possibilities for which were proposed and examined in the earlier consideration of implementation and maintenance provisions, that may be the most important novel source of new and reconditioned arms control instruments and provisions. Such innovation may offer the best hope for future improvement of the promise and prospects of arms control. Herman Kahn wrote in 1960 that "the tools actually or potentially available to the analyst, planner, and decision-maker, both organization and technical, are many times better than anything . . . before. It is just barely possible that with determined efforts by large numbers of responsible people we can achieve enough to make a signicant difference."[6]

This study has recognized that arms-control making is different from war making, peace making, alliance making, and international-organization making, but it has suggested that arms-control making will share characteristics with each of these and that each of these may be an alternate and sometimes preferable way of attaining objectives that arms control might serve. For arms control to be an able and attractive available servant of those objectives, it must be a servant appreciated by advocates, developed by analysts, and proposed by policy makers. Advocacy, analysis, and policy making can benefit by this and further development of arms control theorizing and analysis; the resulting arms control will make a significant difference in international affairs.

[5]HERO, *Study "Riposte": Responses to Violations of Arms Control and Disarmament Agreements* (Washington, D.C.: HERO for the U.S. Arms Control and Disarmament Agency, 1964), pp. 143–144.

[6]Herman Kahn, "The Nature and Feasibility of War and Deterrence," P-1888 RC. (Santa Monica, Calif.: RAND Corporation, 1960), p. 46.

Bibliography

Abel, Elie, *The Missile Crisis*. Philadelphia: Lippincott, 1966.

Abshire, David M., and Richard V. Allen (eds.). *National Security: Political, Military, and Economic Strategies in the Decade Ahead*. New York: Praeger, 1963.

Anderson, H. H. (ed.). *Creativity and Its Cultivation*. New York: Harper & Row, 1959.

Arrow, Kenneth. *Social Choice and Individual Values*. 2d ed. New York: Wiley, 1963.

Ash, Maurice A. "An Analysis of Power, with Special Reference to International Politics," *World Politics*, 3 (1950), pp. 218–237.

Balogh, Thomas. *Unequal Partners*. Vol. 1: "The Theoretical Framework." Oxford: Blackwell, 1963.

Barron, Frank. *Scientific Creativity*. New York: Wiley, 1963.

Batten, James K. *Arms Control and the Problem of Evasion*. Research Monograph, no. 14. Princeton, N.J.: Center of International Studies, 1962.

Beaton, Leonard, and John Maddox. *The Spread of Nuclear Weapons*. London: Chatto & Windus, 1962; New York: Praeger, 1962.

Beaufre, André. *An Introduction to Strategy*. New York: Praeger, 1965.

Bechhoefer, Bernard. *Postwar Negotiations for Arms Control*. Washington, D.C.: Brookings, 1961.

Bell, Daniel. "Twelve Modes of Prediction—A Preliminary Sorting of Approaches in the Social Sciences," *Daedalus,* Summer (1964), pp. 845–880.

Bendix, Reinhard. *Nation-Building and Citizenship*. New York: Wiley, 1964.

Benoit, Emile, and Kenneth E. Boulding (eds.). *Disarmament and the Economy*. New York: Harper & Row, 1963.

Berelson, Bernard and Gary A. Steiner. *Human Behavior*. New York: Harcourt, 1964.

Black, Duncan. *Theory of Committees and Elections*. New York: Cambridge University Press, 1958.

————. "On the Rationale of Group Decision Making," *Journal of Political Economy*, 56 (1948), pp. 22–34.

Bloomfield, Lincoln P. *The Politics of Arms Control: Troika, Veto, and International Institutions*. Washington, D.C.: Institute for Defense Analyses, 1961.

———— (ed.) *International Military Forces*. Boston: Little, Brown, 1964.

————. "Arms Control and World Government," *World Politics*, 14 (1962), pp. 633–645.

Boggs, Marion W. *Attempts to Define and Limit "Aggressive Armament" in Diplomacy and Strategy*. Vol. 16, no. 1, University of Missouri Studies. Columbia, Mo.: University of Missouri Press, 1941.

Bornstein, Morris. "Economic Sanctions as Responses to Arms Control Violations," *Journal of Arms Control*, 1 (1963), pp. 203–218.

Boulding, Kenneth E. *The Image: Knowledge in Life and Society*. Ann Arbor, Mich.: University of Michigan Press, 1956.

————. *Conflict and Defense: A General Theory*. New York: Harper & Row, 1962.

————. "National Images and International Systems," *Journal of Conflict Resolution*, 3 (1959), pp. 120–131.

————. "Towards a Pure Theory of Threat Systems," *American Economic Review*, 53 (1963), pp. 424–434.

Brennan, Donald (ed.). *Arms Control, Disarmament, and National Security*. New York: Braziller, 1961.

Brierly, James. *The Basis of Obligation in International Law, and Other Papers*. New York: Oxford University Press, 1958.

Bright, James R. *Research, Development, and Technological Innovation*. Homewood, Ill.: Irwin, 1964.

Brodie, Bernard. *Strategy in the Missile Age*. Princeton, N.J.: Princeton University Press, 1959.

————. "Military Demonstration and Disclosure of New Weapons," *World Politics*, 5 (1953), pp. 281–301.

————, and Fawn Brodie. *From Crossbow to H-Bomb*. New York: Dell, 1962.

Brown, Neville. *Nuclear War. The Impending Strategic Deadlock*. New York: Praeger, 1965.

Buchan, Alastair, and Philip Windsor. *Arms and Stability in Europe*. London: Chatto & Windus, 1963.

Bull, Hedley. *Control of the Arms Race.* London: Weidenfeld and Nicolson, 1961.

Burin, Frederic S. "The Communist Doctrine of the Inevitability of War," *American Political Science Review,* 57 (1963), pp. 334–354.

Burns, Arthur L. "A Graphical Approach to Some Problems of the Arms Race," *Journal of Conflict Resolution,* 3 (1959), pp. 326–342.

Burton, John. *Peace Theory.* New York: Knopf, 1962.

Burton, John W. "Recent Developments in the Theory of International Relations," in *Yearbook of World Affairs, 1964.* London: Stevens, 1964, pp. 213–229.

Calvocoressi, Peter. *World Order and New States.* London: Chatto & Windus, 1962.

Carlston, Kenneth S. *Law and Organization in World Society.* Urbana, Ill.: University of Illinois Press, 1962.

Clark, Grenville, and Louis B. Sohn. *World Peace Through World Law,* 2d ed. Cambridge, Mass.: Harvard University Press, 1960.

Claude, Inis. *Power and International Relations.* New York: Random House, 1962.

Corbett, J. P. *Europe and the Social Order.* Leyden: Sythoff, 1959.

Cordier, A. W., and W. Foote (eds.). *The Quest for Peace: The Dag Hammarskjold Memorial Lectures.* New York: Columbia University Press, 1965.

Crandall, Samuel B. *Treaties: Their Making and Enforcement.* 2d ed. Washington, D.C.: John Byrne, 1916.

Dallin, Alexander, et al. *The Soviet Union and Disarmament: An Appraisal of Soviet Attitudes and Intentions.* New York: Praeger, 1964.

Davison, William P. *Power—The Idea and Its Communication.* P-1869. Santa Monica, Calif.: RAND Corporation, 1959.

———, M. Kalkstein, and C. Hohenemser. *The Nth Country Problem and Arms Control.* Washington, D.C.: National Planning Association, 1960.

Dean, Arthur. *Test Ban and Disarmament.* New York: Harper & Row, 1966.

Deutsch, Karl W., and J. David Singer. "Multipolar Power Systems and International Stability," *World Politics,* 16 (1964), pp. 390–406.

De Visscher, Charles. *Theory and Reality in Public International Law.* Translated by P. E. Corbett. Princeton, N.J.: Princeton University Press, 1957.

Dinerstein, H. S., Leon Gouré, and Thomas Wolfe (trans.). *Soviet Military Strategy.* V. D. Sokolovskii (ed.), The RAND Corporation (trans.). Englewood Cliffs, N.J.: Prentice-Hall, 1963.

Downs, Anthony. *An Economic Theory of Democracy*. New York: Harper & Row, 1957.

Dunn, Frederick S. *War and the Minds of Men*. New York: Harper & Row, 1950.

Earle, Edward M. (ed.). *Makers of Modern Strategy*. Princeton, N.J.: Princeton University Press, 1941.

Easton, David. *The Political System*. New York: Knopf, 1953.

————. *A Framework for Political Analysis*. Englewood Cliffs, N.J.: Prentice-Hall, 1965.

Economist Intelligence Unit. *The Economic Effects of Disarmament*. London: Economist Intelligence Unit, 1963.

Emmet, Dorothy. *Function, Purpose, and Powers*. London: Macmillan, 1958.

Etzioni, Amitai. *Winning Without War*. Garden City, New York: Doubleday (Anchor), 1965.

Farquharson, Robin. "Sincerity and Strategy in Voting," mimeographed paper, Nuffield College, Oxford, n.d.

Farrell, R. Barry (ed.). *Approaches to Comparative and International Politics*. Evanston, Ill.: Northwestern University Press, 1966.

Finkelstein, Lawrence S. "Arms Inspection," published as *International Conciliation*, no. 540, November, (1962).

Fisher, Roger (ed.). *International Conflict and Behavioral Science: The Craigville Papers*. New York: Basic Books, 1964.

Fox, W. T. R. (ed.). *Theoretical Aspects of International Relations*. South Bend, Ind.: University of Notre Dame Press, 1959.

Friedmann, Wolfgang. *Changing Structure of International Law*. New York: Columbia University Press, 1964.

Friedrich, C. J. (ed.). *Rational Decision*. New York: Atherton, 1964.

Frisch, David H. (ed.). *Arms Reduction: Program and Issues*. New York: Twentieth Century, 1961.

Fuller, J. F. C. *The Conduct of War: 1789–1961*. London: Eyre & Spottiswoode, 1961.

Geldard, Frank A. (ed.). *Defense Psychology*. Proceedings of a Symposium held in Paris, 1960. New York: Pergamon Press for NATO, 1962.

Gibson, Quentin. *The Logic of Social Enquiry*. London: Routledge, 1960.

Gilpin, Robert. *American Scientists and Nuclear Weapons Policy*. Princeton, N.J.: Princeton University Press, 1962.

Goffman, Erving. *Behavior in Public Places*. New York: Free Press, 1962.

————. "On Face-Work," *Psychiatry,* 18 (1955), p. 229.

Gouré, Leon. "Notes on the Second Edition of Marshal V. D. Sokolovskii's *Military Strategy."* RM-3872-PR. Santa Monica, Calif.: RAND Corporation, 1964.

Green, Philip. "Method and Substance in the Arms Debate," *World Politics,* 16 (1964), pp. 642–667

Gruber, H., et al. *Contemporary Approaches to Creative Thinking.* New York: Atherton, 1962.

Haas, Ernst B. *Beyond the Nation-State: Functionalism and International Organization.* Stanford, Calif.: Stanford University Press, 1964.

————. "The Balance of Power: Prescription, Concept, or Propaganda," *World Politics,* 5 (1953), pp. 442–477.

————, and Allen S. Whiting. *Dynamics of International Relations.* New York: McGraw-Hill, 1956.

Hahn, Walter F. *Internal Motives for Soviet Secrecy.* Washington, D.C.: Institute for Defense Analyses, 1963.

Halle, Louis J. "On Teaching International Relations," *Virginia Quarterly Review,* 40 (1964), pp. 11–25.

Halperin, Morton H. *Limited War in the Nuclear Age.* New York: Wiley, 1963.

————. *China and the Bomb.* New York: Praeger, 1965.

————. "A Proposal for a Ban on the First Use of Nuclear Weapons," *Journal of Arms Control,* 1 (1963), pp. 112–123.

Hammond, Paul Y. "Some Difficulties of Self-Enforcing Arms Agreements," *Journal of Conflict Resolution,* 6 (1962), pp. 103–115.

Hanrieder, Wolfram F. "Actor Objectives and International Systems," *Journal of Politics,* 27 (1965), pp. 109–132.

Hekhuis, D. J., C. G. McClintock, and A. L. Burns (eds.). *International Stability: Military, Economic and Political Dimensions.* New York: Wiley, 1964.

Henkin, Louis. *Arms Control and Inspection in American Law.* New York: Columbia University Press, 1958.

———— (ed.). *Arms Control: Issues for the Public.* Englewood Cliffs, N.J.: Prentice-Hall for the American Assembly, 1961.

Herzog, Arthur. *The War-Peace Establishment.* New York: Harper & Row, 1964.

Hindmarsh, Albert E. *Force in Peace: Force Short of War in International Relations.* Cambridge, Mass.: Harvard University Press, 1933.

Historical Evaluation and Research Organization. *Study "Riposte": Re-*

sponses to Violations of Arms Control and Disarmament Agreements. Washington, D.C.: HERO for the U.S. Arms Control and Disarmament Agency, 1964.

Hitch, Charles J., and R. N. McKean. *Economics of Defense in the Nuclear Age*. Cambridge, Mass.: Harvard University Press, 1961.

Hoffmann, Stanley H. "International Systems and International Law," *World Politics,* 14 (1961), pp. 205–237.

——— (ed.). *Contemporary Theory in International Relations*. Englewood Cliffs, N.J.: Prentice-Hall, 1960.

Huntington, Samuel P. *The Common Defense*. New York: Columbia University Press, 1961.

———. "Arms Races: Prerequisites and Results," in C. J. Friedrich and S. Harris (eds.), *Public Policy, 1958*. Cambridge, Mass.: Harvard University Press, 1959, pp. 41–86.

Ikle, Fred C. *How Nations Negotiate*. New York: Harper & Row, 1964.

———. "After Detection—What?" *Foreign Affairs,* January (1961), pp. 208–220.

———. *Alternative Approaches to the International Organization of Disarmament*. Santa Monica, Calif.: RAND Corporation, 1961.

———. "Arms Control and Disarmament," *World Politics,* 14 (1962), pp. 713–722.

Institute for Defense Analyses. *Verification and Response in Disarmament Agreements*. The Woods Hole Summer Study 1962 produced under contract with the U.S. Arms Control and Disarmament Agency. Washington, D.C.: Institute for Defense Analyses, 1962.

Institute for Strategic Studies. *The Military Balance*. London: Institute for Strategic Studies, (annual).

International Sociological Association. *The Nature of Conflict: Studies on the Sociological Aspects of International Tensions*. Paris: UNESCO, 1957.

Jessup, Philip, and Howard J. Taubenfeld. *Controls for Outer Space and the Antarctic Analogy*. New York: Columbia University Press, 1959.

Joint Publications Research Service. *Military Strategy: A Comparison of the 1962 and 1963 Editions*. Washington, D.C.: U.S. Department of Commerce, 1963.

Journal of Arms Control, vol. 1 (1963–1964).

Jouvenel, Bertrand de. *The Pure Theory of Politics*. New York: Cambridge University Press, 1963.

Joynt, C. B. "Arms Races and the Problem of Equilibrium," in *Yearbook of World Affairs 1964,* London: Stevens, 1964, pp. 23–40.

Kahn, Herman. *On Thermonuclear War.* Princeton, N.J.: Princeton University Press, 1961.

——. *Thinking about the Unthinkable.* New York: Horizon Press, 1962.

——. *On Escalation: Metaphors and Scenarios.* New York: Praeger, 1965.

——. "The Nature and Feasibility of War and Deterrence." P-1888 RC. Santa Monica, Calif.: RAND Corporation, 1960.

Kaplan, Morton A. *System and Process in International Politics.* New York: Wiley, 1957.

——, and Nicholas deB. Katzenbach. *The Political Foundations of International Law.* New York: Wiley, 1961.

Kaufmann, William W. *The McNamara Strategy.* New York: Harper & Row, 1964.

Kecskemeti, Paul. *Strategic Surrender.* Stanford, Calif.: Stanford University Press, 1958.

Kent, Col. Glenn A. "On the Interaction of Opposing Forces under Possible Arms Agreements," *Occasional Papers in International Affairs,* no. 5. Cambridge, Mass.: Harvard University Center for International Affairs, 1963.

King-Hall, Stephen. *Defence in the Nuclear Age.* London: Gollancz, 1958.

——. *Common Sense in Defence.* London: K-H Services, 1960.

——. *Power Politics in the Nuclear Age: A Policy for Britain.* London: Gollancz, 1962.

Kissinger, Henry A. *Necessity for Choice.* Garden City, New York: Doubleday (Anchor), 1962.

Knorr, Klaus. *The War Potential of Nations.* Princeton, N.J.: Princeton University Press, 1956.

——, and Thornton Read (eds.). *Limited Strategic War.* New York: Praeger, 1962.

——, and Sidney Verba. *The International System.* Princeton, N.J.: Princeton University Press, 1961.

Lall, Arthur J. *Negotiating Disarmament: The Eighteen Nation Disarmament Conference: The First Two Years, 1962–1964.* Cornell Research Papers in International Studies, no. 2. Ithaca, New York: Cornell Center for International Studies, 1964.

Lall, Betty. "Disarmament Policy and the Pentagon," *Bulletin of the Atomic Scientists,* September (1964), pp. 37–40.

Lasswell, Harold D. *Future of Political Science.* New York: Atherton, 1963.

Levine, Robert A. *The Arms Debate*. Cambridge, Mass.: Harvard University Press, 1963.

———. "Unilateral Initiatives: A Cynic's View," *Bulletin of the Atomic Scientists,* 19 (1963), pp. 22–25.

Liddell-Hart, B. H. *Strategy*. 2d. 1 rev. ed. New York: Praeger, 1967.

Lindblom, Charles E. *Intelligence of Democracy: Decision Making through Mutual Adjustment*. New York: Free Press, 1965.

———. "Policy Analysis," *American Economic Review,* 48 (1958), pp. 298–312.

———. "The Science of Muddling Through," *Public Administration Review,* 19 (1959), pp. 79–88.

Lindsay, Michael. *Is Peaceful Coexistence Possible?* East Lansing, Mich.: Michigan State University Press, 1960.

Liska, George. *The New Statecraft: Foreign Aid in American Foreign Policy*. Chicago: University of Chicago Press, 1960.

———. *Nations in Alliance*. Baltimore: Johns Hopkins Press, 1962.

———. "Continuity and Change in International Systems," *World Politics,* 16 (1963), pp. 118–136.

Luard, Evan. *Peace and Opinion*. New York: Oxford, 1962.

———. (ed.). *The Cold War*. New York: Praeger, 1965.

———. (ed.). *First Steps to Disarmament: A New Approach to the Problems of Arms Reductions*. London: Thames & Hudson, 1965.

McClelland, Charles. *Theory and the International System*. New York: Macmillan, 1966.

McGuire, Martin C. *Secrecy and the Arms Race*. Cambridge, Mass.: Harvard University Press, 1965.

McNair, Arnold Duncan (Lord). *The Law of Treaties*. New York: Oxford University Press, 1961.

McNamara, Robert S. *Statement of the Secretary of Defense before the House Armed Services Committee, Jan. 30, 1963*. Washington, D.C.: Department of Defense, 1963.

McWhinney, Edward. *"Peaceful Coexistence" and Soviet-Western International Law*. Leyden: Sythoff, 1964.

Manning, C. A. W. *The Nature of International Society*. London: London School of Economics and Political Science, 1962.

Marshall, Charles Burton. *The Limits of Foreign Policy*. New York: Holt, Rinehart and Winston, 1954.

———. "Hide and Seek: Dour Thoughts on Inspection," *The New Republic,* Nov. 24 (1962), pp. 14–17. Reproduced in a pamphlet entitled *Cuba: Thoughts Prompted by the Crisis* by the Washington Center of Foreign Policy Research, Washington, D.C., 1962.

Martin, Laurence W. "Disarmament: An Agency in Search of a Policy," *The Reporter,* July 4 (1963), pp. 22–26.

Masters, Roger D. "World Politics as a Primitive Political System," *World Politics,* 16 (1964), pp. 595–619.

Melman, Seymour. *The Peace Race.* New York: Ballantine, 1961.

———. (ed.). *Inspection for Disarmament.* New York: Columbia University Press, 1958.

———. (ed.). *Disarmament: Its Politics and Economics.* Boston: American Academy of Arts and Sciences, 1962.

Millis, Walter. *And End to Arms.* New York: Atheneum, 1965.

———, and James Real. *The Abolition of War.* New York: Macmillan, 1963.

Nicolson, Harold. *Evolution of Diplomatic Method.* London: Constable, 1954.

———. *Diplomacy.* 3d ed. New York: Oxford University Press, 1963.

Noel-Baker, Philip. *The Arms Race.* Dobbs Ferry, New York: Oceana, 1960.

Novick, David (ed.). *Program Budgeting.* Cambridge, Mass.: Harvard University Press, 1966.

O'Connor, Raymond G. *Perilous Equilibrium: The U.S. and the London Naval Conference of 1930.* Lawrence, Kan.: University of Kansas Press, 1962.

Osgood, Charles E. *Limited War: The Challenge to American Strategy.* Chicago: University Chicago Press, 1957.

———. *An Alternative to War or Surrender.* Urbana, Ill.: University of Illinois Press, 1962.

Parsons, Talcott. "On the Concept of Influence," followed by James S. Coleman, "Comment on 'On the Concept of Influence,' " a comment by Raymond Bauer, and a comment by Parsons on Coleman and Bauer, in *Public Opinion Quarterly,* 27 (1963), pp. 37–92.

Partridge, P. H. "Some Notes on the Concept of Power," *Political Studies,* 11 (1963), pp. 107–125.

Peck, Merton J., and Frederic M. Scherer. *The Weapons Acquisition Process: An Economic Analysis.* Boston: Harvard Graduate School of Business, 1962.

Phelps, John B. "Information and Arms Control," *Journal of Arms Control,* 1 (1963), pp. 44–45.

———, et al. *Accidental War: Some Dangers in the 1960's.* Columbus, Ohio: Mershon National Security Program, June 28, 1960.

Pincus, John. *Economic Aid and International Cost Sharing.* R-431-15A. Santa Monica, Calif.: RAND Corporation, 1965.

Powers, Lt. Col. P. W. *A Guide to National Defense.* New York: Praeger, 1964.

Quade, E. S. (ed.). *Analysis for Military Decisions.* Chicago: Rand McNally, 1965.

Quester, George H. *Deterrence Before Hiroshima.* New York: Wiley, 1966.

———. "Bargaining and Bombing during World War II in Europe," *World Politics,* 15 (1963), pp. 417–437.

Rapoport, Anatol. *Fights, Games and Debates.* Ann Arbor, Mich.: University of Michigan Press, 1960.

———. *Strategy and Conscience.* New York: Harper & Row, 1964.

———. "Lewis F. Richardson's Mathematical Theory of War," *Journal of Conflict Resolution,* 1 (1957), pp. 249–304.

Raymond, Jack. *Power at the Pentagon.* New York: Harper & Row, 1964.

Read, Thornton. *Command and Control.* Princeton, N.J.: Center of International Studies, 1961.

———. *Military Policy in a Changing Political Context.* Princeton, N.J.: Center of International Studies, 1965.

Richardson, Lewis F. *Arms and Insecurity.* Chicago: Quadrangle, 1960.

———. *Statistics of Deadly Quarrels.* Chicago: Quadrangle, 1960.

———. "Generalized Foreign Policy," *British Journal of Psychology Monographs Supplements,* 23 (1939).

Riches, Cromwell A. *The Unanimity Rule and the League of Nations.* Baltimore: Johns Hopkins Press, 1933.

———. *Majority Rule in International Organization: A Study of the Trend from Unanimity to Majority Decision.* Baltimore: Johns Hopkins Press, 1940.

Riesman, David. *The Lonely Crowd.* New Haven, Conn.: Yale University Press, 1950.

Riker, William H. *Theory of Political Coalitions.* New Haven, Conn.: Yale University Press, 1962.

———. "Some Ambiguities in the Notion of Power," *American Political Science Review,* 58 (1964), pp. 341–349.

Rock, Vincent P. *A Strategy of Interdependence.* New York: Scribner, 1964.

Ropp, Theodore. *War in the Modern World.* Durham, N.C.: Duke University Press, 1959.

Rosecrance, Richard N. *Action and Reaction in World Politics.* Boston: Little, Brown, 1963.

——— (ed.). *Dispersion of Nuclear Weapons.* New York: Columbia University Press, 1964.

Rosenau, James N. (ed.). *International Politics and Foreign Policy.* New York: Free Press, 1961.

———— (ed.). *International Aspects of Civil Strife.* Princeton, N.J.: Princeton University Press for the Center of International Studies, 1964.

Royal Institute of International Affairs. *International Sanctions.* New York: Oxford University Press, 1938.

Schelling, Thomas C. *Strategy of Conflict.* Cambridge, Mass.: Harvard University Press, 1960.

————. "International Cost-Sharing Arrangements," *Essays in International Finance,* no. 24. Princeton, N.J.: International Finance Section, Department of Economics and Sociology of Princeton University, 1955.

————. "Arms Control: Proposal for Special Surveillance Force," *World Politics,* 13 (1960), pp. 1–18.

————. "Arms Control Will Not Cut Defense Costs," *Harvard Business Review,* March (1961).

————. "War without Pain, and Other Models," *World Politics,* 15 (1963), pp. 465–487.

————. "Review," *American Economic Review,* 54 (1964), pp. 1082–1088.

————. "Signals and Feedback in the Arms Dialogue," *Bulletin of the Atomic Scientists,* January (1965), pp. 5–10. Also published as "The Role of Communication in Arms Control," in Evan Luard (ed.), *First Steps to Disarmament: A New Approach to the Problems of Arms Reduction.* London: Thames & Hudson, 1965, chap. 11.

————. "Reciprocal Measures for Arms Stabilization," in D. Brennan (ed.), *Arms Control, Disarmament, and National Security.* New York: Braziller, 1961, pp. 167–186.

————, and Morton H. Halperin. *Strategy and Arms Control.* New York: Twentieth Century, 1961.

Schilling, Warner, et al. *Strategy, Politics, and Defense Budgets.* New York: Columbia University Press, 1962.

Schwartz, Richard O., and James C. Miller. "Legal Evolution and Societal Complexity," *American Journal of Sociology,* 70 (1964), pp. 159–169.

Sibley, Mulford. *The Quiet Battle.* Garden City, New York: Doubleday (Anchor), 1963.

Singer, Eugene. "A Bargaining Model for Disarmament Negotiations," *Journal of Conflict Resolution,* 7 (1963), pp. 21–25.

Singer, J. David. *Deterrence, Arms Control, and Disarmament.* Columbus, Ohio: Ohio State University Press for the Mershon Center for Education in National Security, 1962.

————. "Inter-Nation Influence," *American Political Science Review,* 57 (1963), pp. 420–430.

Snyder, Glenn. *Deterrence and Defense.* Princeton, N.J.: Princeton University Press, 1961.

Snyder, Richard, et al. *Foreign Policy Decision-Making.* New York: Free Press, 1962.

Spanier, John W., and Joseph L. Nogee. *The Politics of Disarmament: A Study in Soviet-American Gamesmanship.* New York: Praeger, 1962.

Starnes, Richard. " 'Twilight' talks between U.S. and Red China are frail, polite—and occasionally fruitful," *Houston Chronicle,* Feb. 24 (1965).

Stein, Morris I., and Shirley J. Heinze. *Creativity and the Individual.* New York: Free Press, 1960.

Stevens, Carl M. "On the Theory of Negotiation," *Quarterly Journal of Economics,* 72 (1950), pp. 77–97.

Stockfish, J. A. (ed.). *Planning and Forecasting in the Defense Industries.* Belmont, Calif.: Wadsworth, 1962.

Stone, I. F. "A Hopeful Crisis Story the Government Withholds," *I. F. Stone's Weekly,* 10 (Dec. 10, 1962), pp. 1, 4.

Stone, Jeremy J. "Bomber Disarmament," *World Politics,* 17 (1964), pp. 13–39.

Strachey, John. *On the Prevention of War.* London: Macmillan, 1962.

Szilard, Leo. "Disarmament and the Problem of Peace," *Bulletin of the Atomic Scientists,* 11 (1955), pp. 297–307.

Tate, Merze. *The Disarmament Illusion.* New York: Macmillan, 1942.

————. *The U.S. and Armaments.* Cambridge, Mass.: Harvard University Press, 1954.

Triska, Jan P., and David D. Finley. "Soviet-American Relations: A Multiple-Symmetry Model," *Journal of Conflict Resolution,* 9 (1965), pp. 37–53.

Index

Accession to agreements, 135–136

Accidental War: Some Dangers in the 1960's (Phelps), 34n.

"Adjudication and Enforcement in Arms Control" (Sohn), 141n.

Adjudication of agreements 99, 102, 103–106

Administration of agreements, 100–103

Afghanistan, 152

Africa, 50, 151, 153, 156, 168

"After Detection—What?" (Ikle), 113n., 114n.

"Aims of the Law of Tort, The" (Williams), 123n.

Alteration of agreements, 139–142

Alternative Approaches to the International Organization of Disarmament (Ikle), 96n., 101n., 111n., 141n.

Alternative to War or Surrender, An (Osgood), 76n.

Ambiguity in agreements, 135–136

American Multilateral Nuclear Force (MLF), 169, 172

American Scientists and Nuclear Weapons Policy (Gilpin), 66n.

Antarctica Treaty (1959), 5, 18, 22, 67, 159

Antiballistic missile (ABM), 148, 150

Antisubmarine warfare (ASW), 148, 150

Armaments, 10, 32, 35n.–36n., 56

Armies, as a control force, 116–117

Arms and Insecurity and Statistics of Deadly Quarrels (Richardson), 9n.

Arms control

agreements, 88–97, 124–125, 137–142

approaches to, 59–81

and armament, 32–40

attainment of, 83–97

characteristics of, 8–18

determinants of, 54–142

and economy, 40–41

effects of, 7, 14–15

future of, 143–180

and geography, 40

implementation of, 99–133

inducing reciprocation in, 77–79

institutionalization of, 15–18

maintenance of, 135–144

material conditions of, 27–42

and negotiations, 65–70

policy determinants of, 25–56

and political conditions, 43–56

post-World War II, 18–23

prospects for, 161–180

role of, 3–8

stages of, 59–60

193